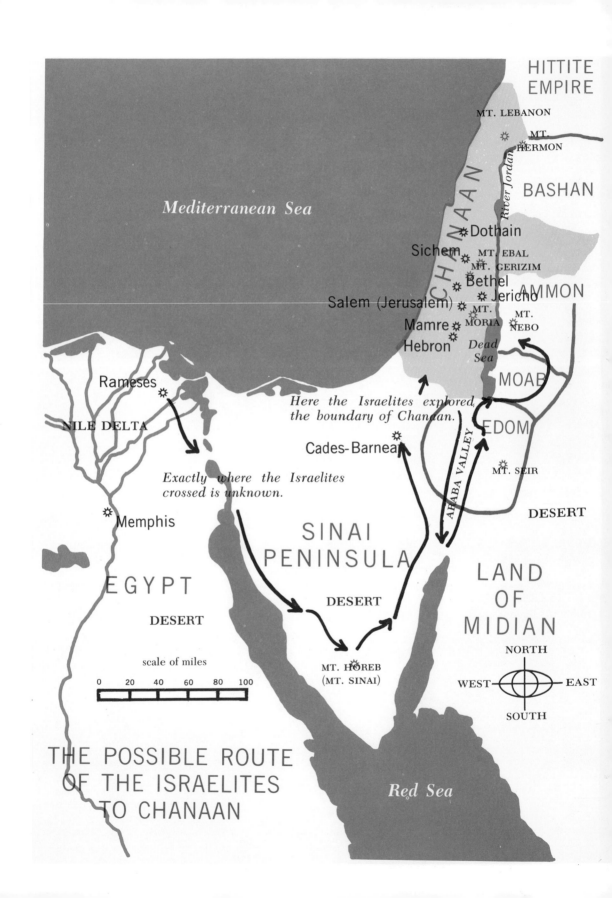

HITTITE
EMPIRE

MT. LEBANON

MT. HERMON

Mediterranean Sea

BASHAN

River Jordan

CHANAAN

Dothain

Sichem   MT. EBAL
         MT. GERIZIM

Bethel
         Jericho

AMMON

Salem (Jerusalem)   MT. MORIA

         MT. NEBO

Mamre

Hebron   *Dead Sea*

MOAB

Rameses

NILE DELTA

Here the Israelites explored the boundary of Chanaan.

EDOM

Cades-Barnea

Exactly where the Israelites crossed is unknown.

ARABA VALLEY

MT. SEIR

Memphis

SINAI
PENINSULA

DESERT

DESERT

LAND
OF
MIDIAN

EGYPT

DESERT

NORTH

scale of miles

0   20   40   60   80   100

MT. HOREB
(MT. SINAI)

WEST — EAST

SOUTH

THE POSSIBLE ROUTE
OF THE ISRAELITES
TO CHANAAN

Red Sea

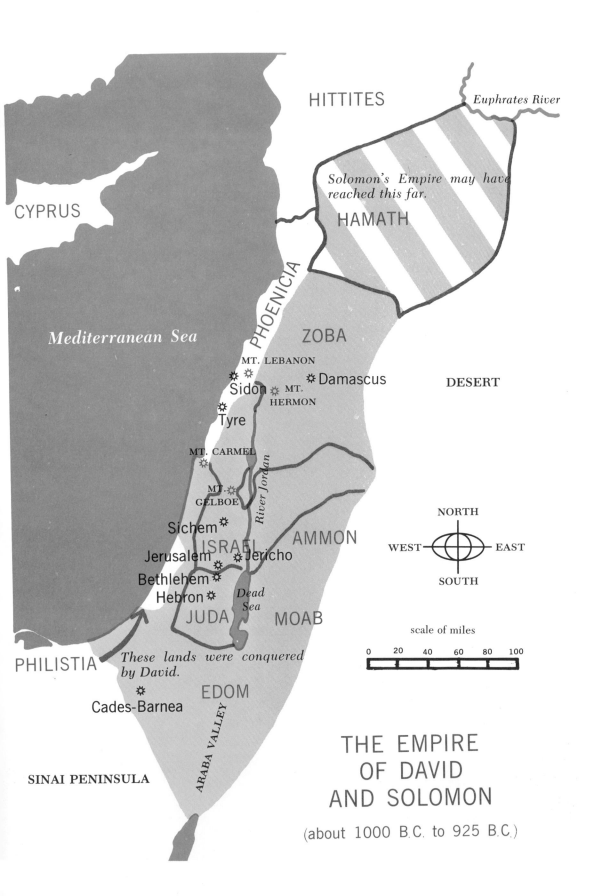

HITTITES

Euphrates River

CYPRUS

*Solomon's Empire may have
reached this far.*

HAMATH

Mediterranean Sea

PHOENICIA

ZOBA

DESERT

MT. LEBANON

Sidon ✸ Damascus

MT.
HERMON

Tyre

MT. CARMEL

River Jordan

MT.
GELBOE

Sichem

ISRAEL

AMMON

NORTH

WEST — EAST

SOUTH

Jerusalem ✸Jericho

Bethlehem

Hebron ✸ *Dead
Sea*

JUDA

MOAB

scale of miles

0   20   40   60   80   100

PHILISTIA

*These lands were conquered
by David.*

EDOM

Cades-Barnea

ARABA VALLEY

THE EMPIRE
OF DAVID
AND SOLOMON

(about 1000 B.C. to 925 B.C.)

SINAI PENINSULA

The
BIBLE
for Children

WRITTEN AND ILLUSTRATED
BY THE DAUGHTERS OF ST PAUL

ST. PAUL EDITIONS

Imprimatur:

✟ Richard Cardinal Cushing
Archbishop of Boston

Library of Congress Catalog Card Number: 68—59068

The Bible and You

The Bible is the most wonderful book in the world, because it is the Book of God. Through the Bible God speaks to each one of us, just as he spoke to the people hundreds of years ago, just as he spoke to our own grandparents and just as he will one day speak to our grandchildren. His message is always the same — a message of his love for us and his desire to save us. That is why he sent his own Son to give his life for us and to teach us how to live, so that one day he can share with us the happiness of his kingdom.

God's message is always the same message of saving love, but the stories he tells us in the Bible are always new. No matter how many times we read them, if we pay attention we will always find something new in them, and we will better understand how God looks after everyone in his great, loving plan, which we call the plan of salvation.

The Bible for Children does not contain the whole Bible, which we hope you will read when you are older. But this book will introduce you to some of the more important happenings in the history of salvation and their meaning. Treasure these stories, for through them God is speaking right to you, just as he spoke to the people of old.

Contents

The Old Testament

The New Testament

The Creation

Thousands and thousands of years ago there was nothing, nothing at all. There were no trees covered with leaves. There was no sun shining in the sky. There was no wind. There was no light to give color to the dawns, and there were no flowers. There were no fish, and there was no sea. There were no stars, no animals, no houses. And there was no earth. Even man was not there. There was nothing, nothing at all. There was only God.

And God had always been there — infinitely powerful, blissfully happy, and immeasurably good.

Out of the greatness of his heart God decided to share his own life and happiness with others. So he began to create.

In the beginning God created the heavens and the earth. The earth was without form and void, and darkness was upon the face of the deep; and the Spirit of God was moving over the waters.

And God said: "Let there be light," and there was light. God saw that the light was good, and he separated the light from the darkness, and called the light Day, and the darkness he called Night. And there was evening and morning, the first day.

And God said: "Let there be a firmament in the midst of the waters, and let it separate the upper from the lower waters." And it was so. And God made the firmament or sky, and separated the waters that were under the firmament from those which were above, and he called the firmament Heaven. And there was evening and morning, the second day.

Then God said: "Let the waters below the heavens be gathered together into one place, and let the dry land appear." And it was so. God called the dry land Earth and the waters that were gathered together he called Seas. And God saw that it was good.

And God said: "Let the earth put forth vegetation, plants yielding seed and fruit trees bearing fruits, in which is their seed, each according to its kind."

And so it was. Then the earth brought forth vegetation, plants yielding seed according to their own kinds, and trees bearing fruits, in which is their seed, each according to its kind. And God saw that it was good. And there was evening and morning, the third day.

Then God said: "Let there be lights in the firmament of the heavens to separate the day from the night, and let them be for signs to mark the seasons, the days and the years, and let there be lights in the firmament of the heavens to shed light upon the earth."

And it was so. And God made the two great lights, the greater light to rule the day, and the lesser light to rule the night; he made the stars also. And God set them in the firmament of the heavens to give light upon the earth, to rule over the day and over the night, and to separate the light from the darkness. And God saw that it was good. And there was evening and morning, the fourth day.

Then God said: "Let the waters bring forth swarms of living creatures, and let birds fly over the earth across the firmament of the heavens." So God created the great sea monsters

and every living creature that moves, with which the waters abound, according to their kinds, and every winged bird according to its kind. And God saw that it was good. And God blessed them saying: "Be fruitful and multiply, and fill the waters in the seas, and let birds multiply on the earth." And there was evening and morning, the fifth day.

And God said: "Let the earth bring forth living creatures according to their kinds: cattle and crawling things and beasts of the earth according to their kinds."

And it was so. And God made all kinds of wild beasts according to their kinds, and the cattle according to their kinds, and everything that creeps upon the ground according to its kind. And God saw that it was good.

Then God said: *"Let us make man in our image and likeness,* and let him have dominion over the fish of the sea and over the birds of the air, and over the cattle, and over all the beasts of the earth, and over every creeping thing that crawls upon the earth." Then the Lord God formed man of dust from the ground, and breathed into his nostrils the breath of life, and man became a living being.

Then the Lord God said: "It is not good that the man should be alone; I will make him a helper like himself." Now the Lord God had already created out of the ground every beast of the field, and every bird of the air. So he brought them to Adam to see what he would call them, because by whatever name the man called every living creature, that was to be its real name. The man named all the cattle, all the birds of the air and all the beasts of the field.

But for the man there was not found a helper like himself. So the Lord God caused a deep sleep to fall upon the man, and while he slept God took one of his ribs and closed up its place with flesh; and the rib which the Lord God had taken from the man he made into a woman, and brought her to Adam.

Then Adam said:

"She is now bone of my bone
And flesh of my flesh:
She shall be called Woman,
Because from Man she has been taken."

Therefore a man leaves his father and his mother and cleaves to his wife, and they become one flesh.

This is the story of the creation which we find in the Bible. It is like a poem, a long and beautiful poem without rhymes.

It is the same account which the divine Story-teller gave to the people of Israel to explain the wonderful work of creation.

The Jewish people liked this simple story, because it was true and easy to understand. From it they learned that *God is the Creator of all. Everything depends entirely on Him. He alone is Almighty God.*

"In the beginning God created heaven and earth." Yes, when there was nothing, nothing at all, God created heaven and earth.

It is true that there was nothing. But God is not like us. We need things in order to make other things. God is all powerful. He can do everything. With his will and with his love he sowed the seed of life in the universe. And life began to throb, and little by little to develop. In the sky millions of stars, planets, comets and meteors began to revolve, at tremendous speed and with perfect regularity.

The waters of the sea were filled with fish of all kinds: tiny fish that could hardly be seen, others that glowed mysteriously in the dark waters, and sharks and whales.

In the ground the first seeds began to sprout. There grew herbs, flowers and trees that made the land ever more lovely.

Everything created by God was beautiful, useful and good. God took pleasure in preparing the home of his creature, man, a home as vast as the universe.

Centuries passed. When all was ready God created man. After he had made his body God gave him a soul and a share in his own life. And the first man was called Adam, which in the Sumerian language means: Father. So Adam, full of joy and gratitude, lived and adored God who had created him.

Then Adam looked at the world around him. What wonders he saw! And all this had been created for him by God so that he might learn to love him more and more.

So Adam began to give names to all the animals. To give anything a name meant taking possession of it, so in this way Adam took possession of his vast home.

But none of the created things resembled him. The sun shone and warmed the earth, but it could not speak, or hear or see. The lion could roar, and was much stronger than the man, but it had no intelligence. The flowers, so pretty in their varied forms and colors, delighted his eyes, but they did not know how to love. Only Adam himself had intelligence and was able to will and to love.

When God had created him he had made him like himself, giving him a share in his own power to will and to love. What were the moon and the stars in comparison with him? Adam might truly have sung with the Psalmist:

You have made him little less than the angels,
And crowned him with glory and honor.
You have given him dominion over the works of
     your hands,
You have put all things under his feet.

Then, in a mysterious way, God created the woman, and brought her to Adam so that together they might form a family. Eve also was intelligent, beautiful and capable of willing and loving. God had given to her the same gifts he had given to Adam.

Now, both together, they were to love God their Creator. They were to adore, praise and thank him, also in the name of the sun, the stars, the animals, the sea, the flowers, and all creatures.

By their work they were to help God to continue his work of creation, by making new, useful and precious discoveries. And they were to love and cherish the children born of their love.

Adam and Eve were perfectly happy. They knew that God loved them and they loved him in return. This is why they were so happy.

We also, like Adam and Eve, are happy because we know that God is our creator and that we belong to him. We lovingly thank him, also in the name of all created things:

Blessed are you, O Lord,
And blessed is your glorious holy name.
Blessed are you in the firmament of heaven,
And to be sung and glorified forever.
Bless the Lord, all works of the Lord,
Sing praise to him and highly exalt him forever.
Bless the Lord, sun and moon,
Sing praise to him and highly exalt him forever.
Bless the Lord, stars of heaven,
Sing praise to him and highly exalt him forever.
Bless the Lord, dews and snows,
Sing praise to him and highly exalt him forever.
Bless the Lord, light and darkness,
Sing praise to him and highly exalt him forever.
Bless the Lord, mountains and hills,
Sing praise to him and highly exalt him forever.
Bless the Lord, all birds of the air,
Sing praise to him and highly exalt him forever.
Bless the Lord, you sons of men,
Sing praise to him and highly exalt him forever.
Give thanks to the Lord, for he is good,
For his mercy endures forever.

O Lord, our Lord,
how glorious is your name over all the earth!
When I behold your heavens, the work of your fingers,
the moon and stars which you set in place —
what is man that you should be mindful of him?
You have made him little less than the angels;
you have given him rule over the works of your hands,
putting all things under his feet.
O Lord, our Lord,
how glorious is your name over all the earth!

Psalm 8

17

Adam and Eve

Adam and Eve, the first man and the first woman, lived in the Earthly Paradise, a very fertile plain, easy to cultivate.

It is very difficult for us today to decide where this place really was. The Jews believed it was in Mesopotamia, which in those times was the most beautiful and fertile country.

God had set Adam and Eve in that land in order that they might take care of it and cultivate it. With his strong arms Adam dug deeply into the soil and prepared it for the seeds he cast into it. These seeds, full of the life which God had put into them, began to sprout, and became little shoots and then leafy trees and bushes. And Adam and Eve enjoyed reaping the fruits of their labors. *Work did not seem to them a heavy toil, but a pleasant pastime.*

They knew that *with their labor they were helping God to complete his work of creation.* In fact, God had set mysterious forces in nature which he wanted man, with his intelligence, to discover and use for the good of all mankind. God wants every man to help him to make the world more and more beautiful, and man more and more happy. So Adam and Eve worked away with joy.

Every day they made marvelous discoveries and learned something new. And they were very happy—happy to live, happy to work, happy to love God and to love each other. They understood and helped each other, and they were happy to think that their union would never come to an end. When God had created them he had said to them: "You will always be joined together." Jesus, the Son of God, was later on solemnly to confirm these words, saying: "A man shall leave his father and mother and be joined to his wife, and the two shall become one flesh."

When God gave Adam and Eve the Earthly Paradise to cultivate, he said to Adam: "You may freely eat of every tree of the garden; but of the tree of the knowledge of good and evil you shall not eat, for in the day that you eat of it you must die." By giving them this command, God made Adam and Eve understand that they would be happy only as long as they obeyed him. The laws he gave them were really only for their own good, and for their own happiness.

By obeying him Adam and Eve were to show God their love and trust, and their dependence on him as children. But one sad day Satan, the devil, tempted them. He was sly and wicked, and he crept closer and closer to them, with the agility and cunning of a serpent. He whispered to Eve: "Did God say: You shall not eat of any tree of the garden?"

And the woman said to the serpent: "We may eat of the fruit of the trees of the garden, but God said: You shall not eat of the fruit of the tree which is in the middle of the garden, neither shall you touch it, lest you die."

But the serpent said to the woman: "You shall not die. For God knows that when you eat of it, your eyes will be opened, and you will be like God, knowing good and evil".

Eve listened attentively. The devil's words dropped one by one into her soul and disturbed her. Gradually she came to believe them, and to think that God had cheated her, that he did not want her to be happy, and that the command he had given her was an obstacle to her happiness.

In an outburst of rebellion and pride Eve disobeyed God's order and persuaded Adam to do the same.

The deceitful devil had convinced them that the fruit of the *tree of knowledge* would make them free and independent, and able to decide for themselves what was good and what was evil without having to depend on God.

But from that dreadful moment sin entered the world like an immense landslide that destroys everything in its path.

Adam and Eve had said 'No' to God. They had gone right away from him, turning their backs on him.

What would happen to flowers if they refused to drink the sap rising from the soil, or if they were to hide their faces from the sunlight? They would wither in a few hours.

Just so, Adam and Eve, separated from God and far from him who was their life, were as if dead.

Their friendship with God had been broken, and they felt poor and lonely. The very worst loneliness is being far from God.

Their minds had become confused and their wills weak.

They were no longer able to love each other as they had done before. *They felt an urgent desire to do evil, and they had a great fear of death.*

If they had not sinned they would not have feared death. God had promised them that they would not die. But now that they were guilty of the sins of pride and disobedience, they knew that they would die. The devil had deceived and ruined them!

They had loved God so much, and now they were afraid of him and ashamed. They had loved to stay in his company, to talk to him, to worship him, praise him and think about him, but now they no longer wanted to see him.

They tried to run away, but God found them and questioned them: "Have you eaten of the tree of which I commanded you not to eat?" The man said: "The woman whom you placed at my side gave me fruit from the tree, and I ate." Then the Lord God said to the woman: "Why have you done this?" The woman answered: "The serpent tricked me, and I ate".

Then God cursed the devil, in the form of the serpent.

Satan had thought that he was the strongest, that with his trickery he had won a great and final victory. And instead he would have to suffer the shameful end of all who are defeated. In ancient times those who had lost a battle were tied to the conquerors' chariots and dragged in the dust and mire through the streets of the city. Satan would have to endure the same fate. This is the meaning of God's curse:

"Because you have done this, cursed are you among cattle, and among all wild animals; upon your belly you shall go, and dust you shall eat all the days of your life. I will put enmity between you and the woman and between your seed and her seed; he shall crush your head and you shall lie in wait for his heel."

To the woman he said: "I will greatly multiply your pain... in pain you shall bring forth children...."

And to Adam he said: "Because you have listened to the voice of your wife, and have eaten of the tree of which I commanded you: You shall not eat of it, cursed is the ground because of you; *in toil you shall eat of it all the days of your life;* thorns and thistles it shall bring forth to you; and you shall eat the plants of the field. In the sweat of your brow you shall eat bread till you return to the ground, for out of it you were taken: you are dust, and to dust you shall return".

Adam and Eve were not cursed but only punished. From that time on they had much to suffer. The earth, cursed by God, would resist man's labors, and only with great difficulty would he be able to make it produce his daily bread.

Eve also, the mother of all the living, would have to suffer much in her motherhood. And she would have to be subject to her husband.

The life of Adam and Eve had completely changed. The justice of God had punished them like a flaming sword. An immense sadness filled their souls. They knew that their sad destiny would be shared by their children and their children's children, and all mankind. All men would receive this sad inheritance from their first father Adam.

But their great sorrow was lightened by a ray of hope. God had said to the devil:

"I will put enmity between you and the woman,
And between your seed and her seed;
He shall crush your head,
And you shall lie in wait for his heel".

As day followed day, these words shone as a bright ray of hope in the hearts of Adam and Eve, for they contained the promise of the Savior to come.

Bless the Lord, O my soul;
and all my being, bless his holy name.
As a father has compassion on his children,
so the Lord has compassion on those who fear him,
For he knows how we are formed;
he remembers that we are dust.

Psalm 102

Cain and Abel

Adam and Eve had sinned and God's punishment struck them in their essential activities: the woman as a mother, the father as a worker. Sin brought upon them many misfortunes which they had not known before.

They had lost their intimacy with God. Their minds and wills had become confused and weak. They were to suffer pain, illness and death. These evils, which were handed on to all men, soon showed themselves in the lives of our first parents and their sons.

Eve bore a son whom she called Cain: "I have given birth to a man-child with the help of the Lord." Abel was born later.

Abel was a keeper of sheep, and Cain a tiller of the ground.... Cain brought to the Lord an offering of the fruit of the ground. Abel brought some of the firstlings of his flock.

God accepted with joy the sacrifices which Abel most lovingly offered him. But those offered by Cain were unwelcome because Cain gave them unwillingly.

God accepts our gifts only if they are accompanied by an intense love.

Cain became irritated by the preference God showed for Abel. He walked with his head bowed and a scowl on his face. He felt jealous of his brother and rebellious towards God. Then God asked him: "Why are you angry, and why are you down-cast? If you do well, will you not be accepted? And if you do not well, sin is couching at the door; its desire is for you, but you must master it".

Therefore, God did not love Abel only. He loved Cain too. That was why he warned him. But Cain preferred to follow the bad impulses of his heart.

He called Abel, invited him to go with him into the country, and killed him.

So the reign of evil, which had begun with the first disobedience, established itself in this dreadful and terrifying manner: a brother killing his own brother! Death, violent and bloody, had entered into the first human family and into the world.

"You are dust," God had said, "and to dust you shall return".

In the earthly Paradise men rebelled against God; here one man fought against another. To this rebellion and strife Jesus would one day oppose a twofold commandment which sums up the whole of the law: "You shall love the Lord your God with all your heart, and with all your soul, and with all your mind.... You shall love your neighbor as yourself".

Cain turned away from the sight of his dead brother. He was frightened. He trembled and wanted to run away. He knew that he had sinned gravely, and he felt full of remorse.

God spoke to him: "Cain, the voice of your brother's blood is crying to me from the ground. And now you are cursed from the ground, which has opened its mouth to receive your brother's blood from your hand. When you till the ground, it shall no longer yield to you its fruit; you shall be a runaway and a wanderer on the earth".

God's voice pierced the heart of Cain, who cried out to him in terror. How could he stay far away from God? How could he stay away from his own land, as a runaway and a wanderer?

Cain said to the Lord: "My punishment is greater than I can bear. This day you have driven me away from the soil; and from your face I shall be hidden; and I shall be a

runaway and a wanderer on earth, and whoever finds me will kill me."

But God reassured Cain and declared that he would severely punish anyone who might hurt him.

Then he set a mark on Cain, the symbol of his protection even over a man who had killed his own brother. Cain was branded with a mark which showed he was a member of a tribe in which the spilling of blood was avenged in a terrible manner, but that mark was to protect him from the revenge of his brothers.

Thus God had avenged the innocent Abel and punished the guilty Cain, whom he had warned in a fatherly manner before the crime was committed. And now, even while inflicting the punishment, God was still merciful.

In front of Cain the earth stretched away dry and barren. He had to begin a new life, full of toil and distress. He was alone, his heart full of remorse, as he wandered wearily towards the unknown future.

Many years passed by. God had given Cain a family, some children and many grandchildren. He had become the chief of a new people. But no descendant of his ever returned to the land of his father. Cain's descendants were very numerous. They were called Cainites and they always lived far from God. God has made some of their names known to us: Henoch, Irad, Mahujael, Mathusael and Lamech.

Lamech surpassed them all in wickedness. He turned against God, challenged him and said that he did not need his help. He himself would carry out his own revengeful purposes, which would be without mercy:
> "I kill a man for wounding me,
> a young man for striking me.
> If Cain is avenged sevenfold,
> truly Lamech seventy-sevenfold".

The wild song of Lamech testifies to the increasing violence of Cain's descendants, about whom the Bible tells us nothing more.

One day Jesus was to command Peter to forgive not "seven times, but seventy times seven".

The Cainites worked hard. They made progress, built towns and invented the first crafts, which gradually made life pleasant and comfortable. The people had good things and could enjoy life. But their prosperity was only earthly. They had shut God out, and so they could not be happy.

Certainly God could not approve of the Cainites' way of living. He could not find among them anyone to whom he could entrust the promise of the Redeemer and the blessing which should have gone to Abel. So God gave Eve another son. Eve accepted him and was consoled and called him Seth, saying: "God has appointed for me another child instead of Abel, whom Cain killed".

Now Adam and Eve were no longer afraid, because the goodness which God had set in their hearts when he created them, was still breathing on this earth, in the fresh youth of their son Seth.

God had replaced Abel with Seth. He bestowed on him his blessing and chose him to bring into the world faith in him and hope in the Savior.

Seth was good like Abel. He became the founder of a new people, who kept their faith in the true God and honored him with public worship.

From Seth descended the great Patriarchs we hear of in the Bible: Noe, Abraham, Isaac, Jacob, Joseph, Moses.... Through these great men, over many centuries, God was to guide his people and prepare them for the Savior's birth. In this way God continued to save men from sin.

O Lord, set a guard before my mouth,
a guard at the door of my lips.
Let not my heart incline to the evil
of engaging in deeds of wickedness.

Psalm 140

The Flood
and
the Tower of Babel

Lamech, a distant descendant of Seth, was faithful to God. He was gladdened by the birth of a son. And his joy was so great that he called the child Noe, which, as the Bible tells us, means "relief" and "consolation".

Out of all the men who inhabited the earth when Noe was born only a few of the descendants of Seth had kept whole their faith in the true God and their love for him. All the others, who had become rich and powerful, had forgotten all about God. They made for themselves idols and monstrous animals and worshiped these as if they were God: the Lord saw that the wickedness of man was great in the earth and that man's every thought and all the inclinations of his heart were only evil.

So God decided to punish man.

But, among so many wicked men, Noe found favor in the eyes of the Lord.... Noe was a good man, blameless in his generation; Noe walked with God. For this reason, when the Lord punished men by means of the flood, he spared Noe and his family.

And God said to Noe: "I have determined to make an end of all flesh; for the earth is filled with violence through them; behold I will destroy them with the earth. Make yourself an ark of resin-wood; make it tight with fiber, and cover it inside and out with pitch".

Then he explained in great detail how Noe was to build the ark, which was to be more or less like a great wooden box, about 500 feet long and 80 feet wide, about 48 feet high, and strong enough to resist the violence of the stormy waters.

When the ark was ready, God ordered Noe to enter it with his wife, his three sons and his sons' wives. He told him to take animals into the ark also—a male and female of every species.

And the rain poured down upon the earth, for forty days and forty nights. The waters rose and bore up the ark with them, and covered even the peaks of the mountains.

All men died, and all animals too. The trees were uprooted and carried away by the flood water; only Noe remained alive, and those who were with him in the ark.

The floods had not covered the whole earth, but only the small part where man then lived. Ancient records of disastrous floods that had covered the plains between the Tigris and the

Euphrates rivers were probably known to the writer of sacred history. In fact, there are Babylonian accounts of the flood which are in some respects similar to the Bible account, although the Bible account clearly does not come from these records and surpasses them in its religious and moral contents.

In the fascinating account given in the Bible, God punishes the unrepentant sinners but spares the just. And so students of sacred history have seen in the historical event of the flood a sublime lesson about the justice and mercy of God.

When the rain stopped, Noe's ark was left floating calmly on the waters.

God waited a little, and then he sent a strong wind which slowly began to dry the land. The ark, which was still rocking on the waters as they subsided, came to rest in the land of Ararat, which today is Armenia. Ararat was perhaps the old name of the land of Armenia.

Noe let the dove fly out of the ark. But the dove came back because it could not find a dry place to perch. The whole land was still submerged.

Noe waited for a few days and then once more let the dove fly out, and in the evening it returned with an olive branch in its beak. So they understood that now the land, dried by the sun's rays, had once more become full of life and color. The first buds were sprouting and all creation was returning to its original splendor. In fact, the third time the dove was sent out it did not come back.

Then Noe understood that the waters had dried up, and God spoke to him: "Go forth from the ark, you and your wife, and your sons and your sons' wives with you. Bring forth with you every living thing that is with you...that they may abound on the earth and be fruitful and multiply upon the earth"

When Noe's large family, followed by all the animals and their families, set foot on the ground, the pious old patriarch was full of gratitude to God, so he thanked him and raised an altar upon which he offered him sacrifices.

God was pleased to accept the sacrifice and promised never again to punish mankind by means of a flood: "While the earth remains, seedtime and harvest, cold and heat, summer and winter, day and night, shall not cease." This was not a covenant or agreement between two parties, but a pledge given freely by God alone. In this way he kept the promise he had made to Noe before the flood: "I will establish my covenant with you."

Now God said: "Behold, I establish my covenant with you and your descendants after you, and with every living creature that is with you, the birds, the cattle, and every beast of the earth with you, as many as came out of the ark. I establish

31

my covenant with you, that never again shall all flesh be destroyed by the waters of a flood, and never again shall there be a flood to destroy the earth." And God said: "This is the sign of the covenant which I make between me and you and every living creature that is with you, for all future generations: I set my bow in the cloud, and it shall be a sign of the covenant between me and the earth"

So from that time on the rainbow has had a symbolic meaning. It stands for peace and the bond of friendship between God and man, which God established after the tremendous punishment of the flood. This pact or pledge was to be followed by the promise God gave *to Abraham:* "I will make you the father of a multitude of nations.... I will establish my covenant between you and me and your descendants after you throughout their generations, as a perpetual covenant, that I may be a God to you and to your descendants after you...and *to the Jewish people:* "This is the blood of the covenant which the Lord has made with you in accordance with all these words of his." These are milestones in the course of sacred history and foreshadow the new covenant, or agreement, that was to be sealed with the blood of Christ.

All men, sharing in the blessing God gave to Noe after the flood, began to live a new and purified life. That purification, which came about by water, is *the symbol of the purification which every man receives in the sacrament of baptism.* Through the water of baptism God saves every soul as he saved Noe.

The sons of Noe, who came out of the ark with him, were called Sem, Ham and Japheth. Noe cultivated a vineyard which produced grapes. He squeezed the juice of the grapes and drank it. He became drunk and unintentionally exposed his body naked. Ham, entering his father's tent, saw him thus, and was so lacking in delicate feeling that he ran to tell his brothers. Then Sem and Japheth respectfully took a cloak, placed it upon their shoulders and, walking backwards, covered their father's nakedness.

When Noe awoke he heard about what had happened and cursed the descendants of Ham. But he blessed Sem and all who were to be born of his line, and he promised Japheth many descendants.

Blessed by God, Sem became the bearer of his message, that is, heir to the true faith and to hope in the Savior. In fact, among his descendants was Abraham, the leader of the chosen people.

Japheth became the father of a very numerous tribe, scattered in various continents and all sharing in the blessing given to Sem.

Ham's descendants lived in the land of Chanaan (the ancient name of Palestine). They were conquered and ruled over by the descendants of Sem when they took possession of the Promised Land upon returning from Egypt.

Many centuries had gone by after the day when Noe blessed Sem and Japheth and cursed the descendants of Ham.

Their families had multiplied and founded many tribes. One of these, a nomadic or wandering tribe, came to a plain in the land of Senaar, that is, in southern Mesopotamia (the region that lies between the two rivers Tigris and Euphrates, and corresponds roughly to modern Iraq) and settled there.

The members of this tribe all spoke the same language and they wished to remain united, perhaps so as not to be obliged to go on wandering from one place to another, as they had done until then. So they decided to erect a monument that would be seen by all.

There was no stone for building in that land, but only clay, so they said: "Come, let us make bricks and burn them thoroughly.... Let us build ourselves a city, and a tower with its top in the heavens, and let us make a name for ourselves, so that we will not be scattered abroad upon the face of the whole earth"

But God had time after time ordered men to multiply and fill the whole earth, so he punished their disobedience by making them no longer able to understand each other's speech. There was such a confusion that they had to stop work and separate.

In this way God showed that he is the Master of the world and of man, and that he fulfills his eternal purposes with wisdom and almighty power.

The tower which the people desired to build was called the Tower of Babel, which, according to the language of those people, means "confusion." In fact, Babel, or Babylonia, which means the Gate of God, actually existed as a city in southern Mesopotamia, and its ruins are still to be seen on the banks of the Euphrates. The Tower of Babel must have resembled those towers which the Mesopotamian cities used to build at that time, and which in the Babylonian language were called "Zigurat." They were formed of seven tiers of terraces built one above another, and connected with ramps and stairways. They had a religious purpose, for the top was always crowned with a little temple.

The account of the Tower of Babel, with its two probable traditional sources, has a double meaning. It illustrates the mercy of God, who wanted men to scatter over the whole earth instead of being confined to the plain of Senaar—and the justice of God, shown in the punishing of man's pride and disobedience.

> *Had not the Lord been with us,*
> *then would the waters have overwhelmed us.*
> *The torrent would have swept over us;*
> *over us then would have swept the raging waters.*
> *Our help is in the name of the Lord*
> *who made heaven and earth.*
>
> *Psalm 123*

Abraham, the Friend of God

About 4,000 years ago Ur, which we now call El-Mugheir, on the shore of the Euphrates, was one of the most ancient and beautiful cities of southern Mesopotamia, the modern Iraq.

In the middle of the city rose a majestic temple with a high tower. There were wonderful palaces adorned with polished bricks, gardens full of flowers and precious pottery. It was a friendly and attractive city. Jewelers, traders and artists lost no chance to come to sell their products in this important economic and religious center.

The inhabitants of Ur did not know the true God. In their magnificent temple they worshiped the moon, which they called "Sin."

In the city of Ur, lived the family of Terah. Terah had three children, who had grown up and were now married. Their names were Abram, Nahor and Aran. The name of Nahor's wife was Milcah and Abram's wife was called Sarai. The third of the brothers had died, leaving a baby boy whose name was Lot.

The whole family formed a tribe of nomads, or wandering herdsmen. The father and the sons had many flocks and herds of sheep and cattle, which were their wealth and also a source of worry to them. When the grass and water began to fail, the tribe had to move on in search of new, well-watered plains.

One day, perhaps because of the war which had broken out at Ur, Terah, the father, decided to go and live at Haran in northern Mesopotamia, nearly 1,000 miles northwest of Ur. He loaded the women and children on strong, patient camels and drove his flocks and herds across the dusty land. Making its way along the river, the caravan set out slowly towards the new home, a fertile plain to the east of the Euphrates.

Many years went by. Old Terah died. His grandson, Lot, had grown up. Abram and Sarai, who loved each other fondly, had no children, and this made them sad.

All the people of the surrounding country worshiped many gods. Abram worshiped a single God and was a just and upright man. One day, while he was quite alone and lost in his thoughts, an extraordinary thing happened to him. The very God whom he worshiped but whom he knew so little, spoke to him:

"Go from your country
and your relatives
and your father's house
to the land that I will show you.
And I will make of you a great nation,
and I will bless you
and make your name great,
so that you will be a blessing.
I will bless those who bless you,
and him who curses you I will curse;
and in you all the nations of the earth
shall be blessed"

These were mysterious and disturbing words.

From this very moment God entered into the life of Abram and into the history of the peoples who would come from him. From now on God would take Abram and his people by the hand and guide them along a new and untried way: the way which leads to salvation.

Abram gave God his willing consent. And he would pass on his faith in the one, all-powerful God to the peoples who were to come from him.

The wonderful story of salvation had begun. Abram arose. God had spoken to him. He was sure of this. "Depart, go to the land I will show you!" What was this land? God had not told him its name.

36

And the words: "I will make of you a great nation" — what could they mean, if he had not even one child to be his heir and in his turn to have many other children who would become an immense nation? And what was the meaning of that promise: "You will be a blessing...in you all the nations of the earth shall be blessed"?

But Abram believed, and set out.

He took with him his wife Sarai, his nephew Lot, his servants, all his herds and wealth, and made his way towards that unknown country.

Along the way Abram's caravan met with other caravans. Rich merchants were traveling towards the best market-places to sell their goods. Other wandering tribes were going out in search of good pastures. Only Abram was going where God had called him.

After the long crossing of the desert, Abram stopped in the region of Chanaan, the Palestine of today. He settled there with his family and his herds, near the city of Sichem, in what is today Samaria; between the mountains of Gerizim and Ebal, where the pastures were more abundant.

A few orders to the servants, and the tents were pitched in the shade of the Oak of Moreh. The women were busy in the black tents woven with goat's hair. The herds were browsing on the grass. From a little hill, Abram was looking at the land to which he had come. And he felt a stranger in a strange land. And he thought: "What will the Lord want of me?" Then he heard a voice: "Abram, to your descendants I will give this land"

It was the voice of God. God had asked him to leave the land of his fathers, and now he promised him that this strange land, inhabited by Chanaanites, was to be the land of his children's children. His heart throbbed with joy, and he raised an altar to the Lord.

Later he moved about twenty miles further to the south and pitched his tents in the valley between the towns of Bethel (today Betein) and Hai, on the hill we know now as et-Tell.

But a terrible dry spell forced Abram to leave that place and to seek shelter in Egypt, the fertile land watered by the

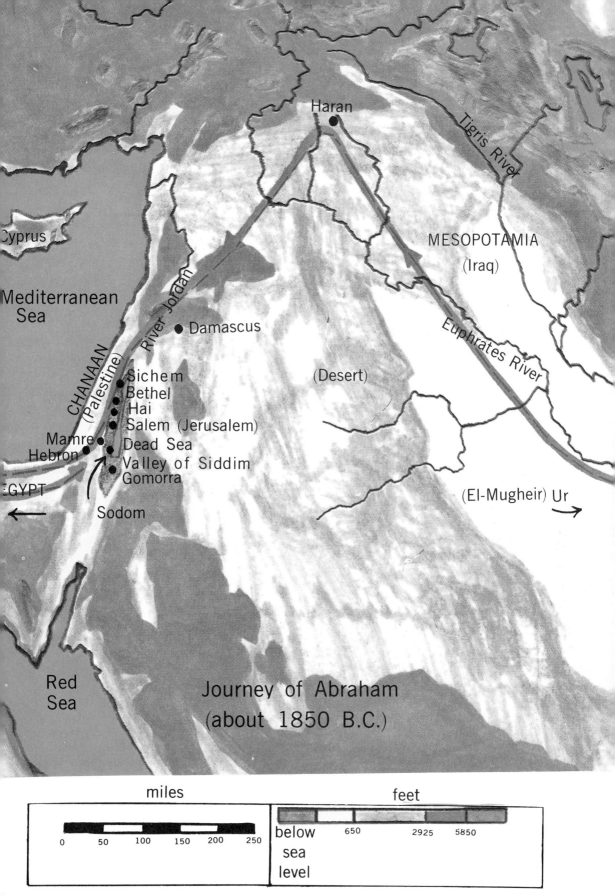

Haran

Tigris River

MESOPOTAMIA
(Iraq)

Cyprus

Mediterranean
Sea

River Jordan

Damascus

Euphrates River

CHANAAN
(Palestine)

Sichem
Bethel
Hai
Salem (Jerusalem)
Mamre
Hebron
Dead Sea
Valley of Siddim
Gomorra
Sodom

(Desert)

(El-Mugheir) Ur

EGYPT

Red
Sea

Journey of Abraham
(about 1850 B.C.)

miles

feet

below
sea
level

0   50   100   150   200   250

650   2925   5850

Nile. On his return he realized that that land could no longer support his family as well as Lot's. The cattle had increased and more than one quarrel had broken out between Lot's herdsmen and his own.

Abram, who loved peace and harmony, could not bear this. He called Lot and said to him: "Let there be no strife between you and me, and between your herdsmen and my herdsmen; for we are close relatives. Is not the whole land before you? Separate yourself from me. If you take the left hand, then I will go to the right; or if you take to the right hand, then I will go to the left"

Lot lifted up his eyes and saw the Jordan valley, as well watered as the land of Egypt. He chose this territory and pitched his tents near the city of Sodom.

But Abram went to dwell by the oaks of Mamre — Ramet el Khalil as we know it today — to the north of Hebron.

Some time later, a war party of eastern kings led by Chodorlahomor, had advanced as far as the lands which were to the south of the Dead Sea, in the valley of Siddim, to subdue all the kings of those cities, who had rebelled against them. After their victory, these kings came back to their own lands, running wild in Sodom and Gomorra and taking goods and prisoners with them. Among the prisoners there was Lot also.

As soon as Abram heard of this, he gathered his fighting men, choosing the best trained warriors among them. He pursued the enemy as far as the northwest of Damascus, defeating the rear guard and freeing Lot with his family.

On his way back, Abram was met and greeted by Melchisedech, king of Jerusalem, which was at that time called Salem. Since he was priest of God Most High, Melchisedech offered God a sacrifice. It was of bread and wine. Then the priest blessed Abram with these words:

> "Blessed be Abram by God Most High,
> maker of heaven and earth;
> and blessed be God Most High,
> who has delivered your enemies
> into your hands"

40

This sacrifice of bread and wine, offered by Melchisedech, king and priest, is the symbol of another sacrifice: that of Jesus, who offers to his Father his own Body and Blood under the species of bread and wine. The 109th psalm says of Jesus: You are a priest forever after the order of Melchisedech.

Since Abram had no child, he had chosen as his heir Eliezer, who was the most trustworthy of his servants. After his death this slave would become his successor.

But God spoke to Abram and said: "Fear not, Abram, I am your shield; your reward shall be very great." But Abram said: "O Lord God, what will you give me, for I continue childless and the heir of my house is Eliezer of Damascus?..." But the word of the Lord came to him: "This man shall not be your heir; your own son shall be your heir." And he brought him outside and said: "Look toward heaven, and count the stars, if you are able to count them.... So shall your descendants be"

This time, too, Abram believed in God's word and God made a covenant, or agreement, with his friend, whom he trusted, and said to him:

"I am God Almighty;
walk before me and be blameless...."

Then Abram fell on his face and God said to him: "Behold, my covenant is with you and you shall be the father of a multitude of nations. No longer shall your name be Abram, but your name shall be Abraham (which means 'Father of a multitude'); for I have made you the father of a multitude of nations. I will make you exceedingly fruitful; and I will make nations of you, and kings shall come forth from you. And I will establish my covenant between me and you and your descendants.... I will give to you, and to your descendants after you, the land you have visited, all the land of Chanaan, for an everlasting possession; and I will be their God.... As for you, you shall keep my covenant, you and your descendants after you, throughout their generations. This is my covenant, which you shall keep.... Every male among you shall be circumcised.... As for Sarai your wife, you shall not call her Sarai, but Sara shall be her name. I will bless her, and moreover I will give you a son by her.... Kings of peoples shall come from her"

The covenant was now established. God Most High had looked down upon Abraham to form a pact of friendship with him.

Abraham was now a new man. He had believed, and God, loving him, had made him more upright and good. His name, which meant "great father," had been changed, and from that time to this he would be called "father of a multitude."

Abraham promised to act as a friend of God and to continue to do everything God would ask of him.

Give thanks to the Lord, sing his praise,
rejoice, O hearts that seek the Lord!
He remembers forever his covenant
which he entered into with Abraham. Psalm 104

The Father of All Believers

Abraham had set up his tents by the Oaks of Mamre, to the north of Hebron.

One day, while he was sitting alone at the door of his tent, he saw three men coming towards him. He ran to meet them and greeted them by bowing to the ground, as was the custom in those days, and invited them to stay with him.

"Permit me to have water brought to you," said Abraham in welcome. "You shall wash your feet and rest in the shade of the tree. I will bring you something to eat. You shall refresh yourselves before you continue on your way."

They replied: "Do as you have said."

Abraham hurried to Sara, who was in the tent, and said to her: "Quick, take three measures of flour and knead it and make some bread." Meanwhile he ran into the oxen's stall and took a young calf and handed it to his servant, who made haste to kill and cook it. Then he brought some milk for the men to drink, and the veal, already cooked. He placed this food before his guests.

While they were eating Abraham stood beside them under the tree. "Where is Sara, your wife?" they asked him.

"She is in the tent," replied Abraham.

One of his guests (who was God himself, whereas the other two were angels) said: "I will surely return to you in a year's time and then Sara, your wife, will have borne a son."

Sara, who was listening inside the tent door, began to laugh as she thought to herself: "That cannot come true—

it is impossible! Abraham and I are already too old to have children."

"Why did Sara laugh?" asked the guest. "In a year's time, when I return to you, Sara will surely have a son. It is the Lord who has decreed it. Is there anything impossible to the Lord?"

About a year later, when Sara became the mother of a fine son, she understood that the travelers told the truth.

Abraham gave his son the name Isaac which, in its complete form, means "May God smile upon me," or "May God look upon me with favor." And Abraham understood more and more that God is faithful to his promises and that he is a powerful and loving God.

On the southwestern banks of the Dead Sea there were, in the days of Abraham, the cities of Sodom and Gomorra. The people living in these cities had become very wicked. The impure sin against nature which is in fact called "sodomy" after the city called Sodom, had become for them something to boast about. Although he still loved the people, God decided to punish them, so that their punishment should serve as a warning to all other peoples.

But before he punished them God thought to himself: "Can I hide from Abraham what I am about to do, seeing that Abraham will be the founder of a great and mighty people, and all nations of the earth will be blessed in him? No, for I have chosen him, so that he may charge his children and his household after him to keep in the way of the Lord by doing what is good and right — so that the Lord may do for Abraham what he has promised him."

Then God said to Abraham: "The screaming against Sodom and Gomorra that reaches my ears is great and their sin is very grave."

But Abraham asked God: "Lord, would you destroy the good with the wicked? Suppose there were fifty good men in that city, would you allow them to perish with the others? Would you not rather forgive the city for the sake of the fifty good men who might be there?... Far be it from you to do such a thing, to treat the good in the same way as the wicked! Shall not the judge of the whole earth deal justly?"

The Lord replied: "If I find fifty good men in the city of Sodom, I will spare the whole city for their sake."

But Abraham replied: "Although I am but dust and ashes — that is, as nothing in your sight — I dare to ask my Lord: If five of these fifty good men were missing, would you destroy the whole city for the lack of those five?"

And the Lord answered: "If I find forty-five I will not destroy it."

Abraham insisted: "And if there were only forty good men?"

"I would not destroy it, for the sake of those forty."

"O Lord, do not be angry with me if I continue to plead with you," said Abraham, "but what if there were only thirty?"

"If I find there only thirty I will not destroy it."

And Abraham said: "Permit me, Lord, still to ask you: if there were but twenty of them?"

And the Lord: "For the sake of those twenty I will not destroy it."

And Abraham said: "Bear with me, Lord, while I ask this only: and if there were only ten?"

And the Lord replied: "For the sake of those ten I will not destroy it"

Abraham's wonderful and heartwarming request helps us to understand that God welcomes prayer on behalf of our fellowmen, and that goodness — even the goodness of a few — may bring about the salvation of many sinners. To Abraham's question, "Lord, would you let the good perish with the bad?" God replied, not with words but with deeds, for he spared the lives of Lot and his family.

This story shows us that in Abraham's time all the people felt closely bound together, in good as in bad, so that in a certain sense the evil done by one was harmful to all, and the good done by one was helpful to all. This close bond of union was to appear in all its greatness in the sacrifice of Jesus. The day would come when the prayer and suffering of one good Man,

Jesus, true God and true Man, would bring about the salvation of the whole world.

Even before the coming of Jesus, God taught the descendants of Abraham that everyone must bear the burden of his own sin: "I will judge you, house of Israel, each one according to his ways".

But in Sodom there were not even ten people judged good in the eyes of God, and so all were punished. Bolts of lightning set fire to the many mineral wells of bitumen and sulphur scattered throughout the region, and the sulphurous fumes covered the whole city, burying it under a fiery rain. Then an earthquake wrecked those cities and the waters of the Dead Sea flowed over them.

The region around the Dead Sea is still dry and barren, and the water of this sea is so salty that no fish or plant can live in it.

Abraham's son Isaac grew up strong and healthy. Having been born after so many years of waiting, he was the joy and hope of his parents. They loved him more than their own lives.

One day God wished to test Abraham to see how much he really loved him, so he called to him: "Abraham!"

And Abraham answered: "Here I am!"

"Take your son, your only son Isaac, whom you love, and go to the district of Moria, and there offer him as a burned offering upon one of the mountains, which I shall point out to you"

Abraham felt his heart breaking with sorrow. God himself had given him his only son. Why did he now wish to take him away? And how could God then keep his word — for he had promised Abraham to make him the father of many peoples — if he now took his son away?

But Abraham knew that everything belongs to God, and that he can ask for anything from his children. Completely resigned to God's will, Abraham prepared to offer the greatest sacrifice of his life.

So Abraham rose early in the morning, saddled his donkey, and took two of his young servants with him, along with his son Isaac. He cut the wood for the burned offering and set out.

On the third day Abraham lifted up his eyes and saw the mountain afar off. He said to his servants: "Stay here with the donkey; I and the lad will go up there and worship, and return to you."

And Abraham took the wood for the burned offering and laid it on the shoulders of his son Isaac, and he took the knife in his hand. So they went on together.

And Isaac said to his father Abraham: "My father!"

And he said: "Yes, my son."

Isaac said: "Here is the wood, but where is the lamb for the burned offering?"

Abraham said: "God himself will provide the lamb for the burned offering, my son."

So they went on together. When they came to the place of which God had told him (a place we cannot identify today, although traditions claim it as the rock upon which the Temple of Jerusalem was built), Abraham set up an altar and bound Isaac his son, and laid him on the wood upon the altar. Then he put out his hand and took the knife to kill his son. But the angel of the Lord called to him from heaven: "Abraham! Abraham!"

And he said: "Here I am!"

The angel said: "Do not lay your hand on the lad, or do anything to him. For now I know that you fear God, seeing you have not withheld your son, your only son, from me."

Then Abraham lifted up his eyes and saw a large male sheep, or ram, with its curved horns caught in a bush. He took it and offered it up as a burned offering, instead of his son. And he called the name of that place *The Lord will provide*

So Abraham understood that God did not want the sacrifice of human victims, as was the cruel custom of the pagan peoples. He had asked him for this sacrifice only in order to

test his faith and obedience. And Abraham was more than ever convinced that God was watching over him.

This great patriarch Abraham was the man chosen by God to hand down faith in the one almighty God to all the peoples who were to come after him.

To believe means to accept the word of God as it is presented to us by the Bible and the Church, and to do everything God asks of us.

Abraham believed in God and did all that God asked of him, even at the cost of the greatest sacrifices. About 1800 years after the death of Abraham, Jesus spoke to the Jews about this great patriarch of theirs and said: "Your father Abraham rejoiced that he was to see my day; he saw it and was glad".

With these words Jesus reminded the Jews that Abraham's faith was so great that he was sure that from among his descendants there would be born One who would bring the greatest blessing to mankind: Jesus, the Savior of the world. It was as if Abraham could see Jesus across the centuries.

In the New Testament we are told that by faith Abraham obeyed when he was called to go out, and he went out, not knowing where he was to go; by faith he lived in the land of promise, as in a foreign land, living in tents; by faith Abraham, when he was tested, offered up Isaac, his only son, reasoning that God is able to raise men even from the dead.

Because of his great faith Abraham is the *"father of all believers"* the father of all those who, in every moment of their lives, say "yes" to God.

The plan of the Lord stands forever;
the design of his heart through all ages.
Happy the nation whose God is the Lord.
Our soul waits for the Lord
for in him our hearts rejoice.
May your kindness, O Lord, be upon us
who have placed all our hope in you.

Psalm 123

Jacob

God blessed Isaac as he had blessed his father Abraham. Isaac had two sons, Esau and Jacob. One day the two young men had a fight, and Jacob had to flee for his life. He set out for the home of his uncle, Laban, in the vicinity of distant Haran.

The first night, at sunset, he placed a stone under his head for a pillow and fell asleep. He dreamed.... It seemed that there was a ladder with its base on the ground and its top reaching to heaven; angels of God were ascending and descending on it. Above the ladder was the Lord, who said to Jacob: "I am the Lord God of Abraham and of Isaac! To you and to your descendants I will give this land on which you lie. And your descendants shall be as the dust of the earth.... And behold, I am with you; I will protect you wherever you go, and I will bring you back to this land"

When he rose in the morning, Jacob continued his journey.

He returned to the land of Chanaan many years later, and made peace with his brother Esau. And God gave Jacob a new name: "You shall no longer be called Jacob, but Israel"

As Abraham before him, Jacob, too, firmly believed in the word of God.

Joseph

Together with his sons, Jacob had returned to the land of his fathers—Chanaan. Rachel, his beloved wife, had died in giving birth to Benjamin, and had been buried near Bethlehem

Now they continued on their journey south. To the south was Hebron, one of the most ancient cities of the world, now a small Arab town called El-Kalil, with narrow winding streets and snow white houses crowned with cupolas. Not far from there Jacob set up his tents. Near to the tombs of Sara, Abraham and Isaac, he gathered his strength and courage to go on living.

The sons of Jacob, or Israel, were called Reuben, Simeon, Levi, Juda, Issachar, Zabulon, Dan, Nephthali, Gad, Aser, Joseph and Benjamin. Jacob loved them all, but his favorite son was Joseph. He had a most beautiful tunic made for him, with long sleeves, like those worn by the sons of noblemen. But his other sons were jealous and began to mistreat Joseph.

One night Joseph had a strange dream, which he described to his brothers the next morning. "Listen, while I tell you about my dream. We were in the middle of the field, binding the sheaves of grain. All at once my sheaf rose up and stood upright, and your sheaves gathered around it and bowed down to my sheaf."

His brothers said to him: "Do you imagine that you will be our king and rule over us?"

Some time after this Joseph told his father and brothers about another dream. This time he had dreamed that the sun,

the moon and eleven stars had bowed down before him. His father scolded him: "What is the meaning of this dream of yours? Do you suppose that I...and your brothers will bow to the ground before you?"

His brothers became more and more jealous of him but his father, who loved him dearly, pondered over these sayings.

Jacob's tribe, like Abraham's, was a tribe of shepherds. When the flocks had eaten the grass of the pastures around their village of tents, the shepherds took down the tents and moved off in search of fresh grazing grounds.

One day Joseph's brothers went to look for new pastures in the valley of Sichem, where Jacob had some property.

The village of Sichem, today known as Tell-el-Balata, is located forty miles to the north of Jerusalem, along a road still used today. Some time after his sons' departure, Jacob decided to send Joseph to find them. He called him and said: "You know that your brothers have gone to the pastures at Sichem. Go and see how they are, and how the flock is doing, and then come back to tell me."

Joseph set out from Hebron, but when he arrived at Sichem he found that his brothers had gone about twenty-three miles farther north, to Dothain, the modern Tell-Dothan, situated on the great caravan route that runs from Syria to Egypt.

When his brothers saw Joseph approaching, a traveler having shown him the way, they said to each other: "Here comes the dreamer! Now let us kill him and throw him into a well; then we will say that a wild beast has devoured him."

But the oldest brother, Reuben, rescued him from their hands, saying: "Let us not kill him. Do not shed his blood. Throw him into that well we saw in the wilderness, but do not lay your hands on him."

So they took Joseph and stripped him of his fine tunic and threw him into the well, which had no water in it. Then, covering the well, they sat down and began to eat. All at once, as they looked up, they saw a caravan of merchants coming from the direction of Gilead, to the east of the Jordan. The merchants were going to Egypt to sell their fragrant gum, balm and myrrh, which were used in medicine and for the preserving of dead bodies.

Juda said to his brothers: "What do we gain by killing our brother and concealing his blood? Come, let us sell him to the merchants and avoid killing him with our own hands, as he is our brother and our own flesh and blood."

They all agreed to this. They drew Joseph up out of the well and sold him for twenty silver shekels, that is, for ten

shekels less then the price of a young slave. Then they dipped the long-sleeved tunic in the blood of a goat and gave it to one of their servants, who took it to Jacob.

The servant said: "Look, we have found this. Is it not your son's tunic?"

"It is my son's tunic," said the father, weeping. "A wild beast has devoured him"

Meanwhile the merchants' caravans arrived in Egypt. There Joseph was sold again, this time as a slave to Phutiphar, one of the Pharao's officers commanding the king's guard and the royal executioners.

But God, who *"in everything works for good with those who love him"* (Romans 8:28) — and this is the central thread of the story of Joseph — protected the young slave, who prospered in all he did. He won the respect of Phutiphar, took him as his personal attendant and then placed him in charge of his house and of all his possessions.... And God blessed the Egyptian's house, for the sake of Joseph

Now Joseph was very good-looking. One day Phutiphar's wife tried to persuade him to act dishonorably. The young man hotly refused and said to her frankly: "How could I do this dishonorable thing and sin against God?"

But the bad-intentioned woman told everyone that the slave had tried to harm her. And she told this lie to her husband, who believed her and had Joseph shut up in the dungeon where the king's prisoners were confined. But the Lord was with Joseph (Genesis 39:21), and caused him to find favor with the keeper of the prison, who placed him in charge of all the other prisoners.

One day, for some misdoing of which the Bible does not inform us, there came to be imprisoned in the same place the Pharao's chief butler and chief baker. The former had had the task of watching over whatever was brought for the king to eat or drink, in order to prevent any attempt to poison him; the latter had prepared the bread, cakes and pies for the royal table. After some time the two new prisoners both had dreams which left them feeling puzzled.

54

"Why do you both look so sad today?" Joseph asked them the next morning.

"We have both had dreams, and there is no one to interpret them for us," they said.

"Is God not able to interpret them? Tell me what you have dreamed"

One after the other the two prisoners described their dreams, and Joseph explained their meaning to them, a meaning that was later shown to be true by what happened: the head baker was hanged, whereas the head butler returned to court, where "he placed the cup in the Pharao's hand."

One night the Pharao himself had a strange dream. He sent for all the wise men and magicians of his kingdom to try to discover its meaning, but none of them could give him any explanation.

Then the chief butler remembered the young Hebrew who had interpreted his own dream to him when he was in prison; he spoke of him to the Pharao, who immediately ordered his release. Then Joseph, dressed in new clothes, came to the Pharao, who had said to him: "I have dreamed a dream and there is no one who can interpret it for me. I have heard that after a dream is retold to you, you can interpret it." Joseph replied: "Not I, but my God, will give the answer, for the good of Pharao."

The Pharao told him: "I dreamed I stood on the banks of the Nile. From the river there came up seven cows, fat and sleek, and they grazed among the reeds; but then there came up seven other cows, poor and very gaunt and thin, such as I had never seen in all the land of Egypt. Then the thin cows devoured the seven fat cows but, after they had devoured them, it was as if they had never eaten them, for they were still as thin as ever. And I woke up.

"I also saw in my dream seven good full ears of corn growing on a single stalk. And after these there sprouted seven thin and withered ears, dried out by the burning wind from the east. And the thin ears of corn swallowed up the seven good ears. I have described these dreams to the wise men, but none of them could explain them to me."

Then Joseph said to the Pharao: "Both your dreams have the same meaning. God is warning the Pharao of what he is about to do.... I will explain: there will now be seven years of very good harvests in the whole land of Egypt. But these will be followed by seven years of famine, and all the plenty will be nothing but a memory in Egypt because all the people will go hungry. So the Pharao must find a wise and careful man and set him at the head of the government of Egypt. He must appoint supervisors throughout the land to collect a fifth part of all the crops during the seven years of plenty.... These provisions, held in storage, will be used for the land during the seven years of famine that will follow; in this way the people will not be destroyed by hunger."

The Pharao was pleased with Joseph's advice. He said to his servants: "Can we ever find another man as good as this one, as full of the spirit of God?" Then turning to Joseph, he added: "Since God has revealed all this to you, there is no one as wise and careful as you. You shall be the supervisor of my house, and all my people shall be at your orders; only by reason of my kingly power shall I be greater than you.... I set you over the whole land of Egypt".

Then he took the ring from his finger and placed it upon Joseph's finger as a sign of the authority he was giving to him. He robed him in a fine linen tunic and put a gold chain about his neck. Then he made him get into his chariot and ride through the whole land. So at thirty years of age Joseph was Viceroy of Egypt.

God had not spared him suffering. But the young Hebrew had always believed that God is present in everything that happens to us, whether it be joyful or sad, and that God provides for his children and leads them by the hand in order to fulfill his purposes.

The years passed. During the famine, Joseph's brothers went twice into Egypt to buy grain. Joseph recognized them, but they did not recognize him. The second time they came, Joseph could no longer hide his affection, and he exclaimed: "I am Joseph." Then he hugged them and told them to go

back to Jacob, their father, and to ask him to come and live in Egypt.

The old patriarch, together with his large family, immediately set out for Egypt.

When Joseph received the news that his father was arriving, he went to meet him and embraced him with tears.

He led his old father and his brothers before Pharao, who received them with great honor and gave them fertile land to live on.

Thus, as a part of God's plan, Israel (Jacob) and his entire family had moved to Egypt. Here again, God did not abandon his chosen ones.

Some time after the death of Jacob, Joseph realized that his own death was also drawing near. He called his brothers and told them: "God will lead you up from this land to the land of Chanaan.... And when you do go up, take my bones along with you"

I love you, O Lord, my strength.
Toward the faithful you are faithful,
toward the wholehearted you are wholehearted.
Humble people you save,
but the proud you bring low.
I will proclaim you among the nations,
and I will sing praise to your name.
Psalm 17

Moses

For several years, Jacob's descendants, whom we call the *Hebrews* or *Israelites*, were very happy in Egypt. Then a new family of Pharaos came into power, and they took the Hebrews to be their slaves. The Hebrews were beaten and treated very cruelly.

It was time for God to deliver his people. He chose a man to be his messenger or *prophet*. That man was Moses. God appeared to him in fire flaming out of a bush. As Moses looked on, he saw that the bush, though on fire, did not burn up. So he decided, "I must go over to look at this marvelous sight and see why the bush is not burned." But God called out to him from the bush, "Moses! Moses!"

Moses answered, "Here I am."

God said, "Come no nearer! Remove the sandals from your feet, for the place where you stand is holy ground. I am the God of your father," he continued, "the God of Abraham, the God of Isaac, the God of Jacob."

Moses hid his face, for he was afraid to look at God. Then the Lord said, "I have seen the suffering of my people in Egypt.... Therefore, I have come down to rescue them from the hands of the Egyptians and lead them out of that land into a good and spacious land, a land flowing with milk and honey. ...Come now! I will send you to Pharao to lead my people, the Israelites, out of Egypt."

The Lord then gave Moses the gift of miracles: "Throw the rod you have in your hand on the ground," he said. Moses obeyed. The rod immediately changed into a snake, and Moses drew away from it. "Take hold of its tail," the Lord said. Moses put out his hand, and laid hold of it, and it became a rod again.

"You will work these miracles that they may believe that it is I who have sent you," said God.

After that, Moses and his brother Aaron went to Pharao and said, "Thus says the Lord, the God of Israel: Let my people go, that they may celebrate a feast to me in the desert."

Proudly Pharao answered, "Who is the Lord, that I should hear his plea to let Israel go? I do not know the Lord; even if I did, I would not let Israel go."

To convince him, Moses worked many miracles in his presence, but, blinded by pride, Pharao would not give in. In fact, he ordered that the Hebrews be treated more cruelly than before. To force Pharao to let his people go, the Lord then sent ten terrible punishments, called the *ten plagues of Egypt.* He said to Moses:

"Pharao's heart is stubborn in refusing to let the people go. Tomorrow morning, when he goes toward the river, present yourself before him on the bank of the Nile, holding in your hand the staff that changed into a serpent. Say to Pharao: 'The Lord, the God of the Hebrews, sent me to you with the message: Let my people go to worship me in the desert. But you have still not listened. The Lord now says: This is how you shall know I am the Lord. I will strike the water of the Nile with the staff that is in my hand, and it shall turn into blood. The fish in the Nile will die, and the river itself shall become so polluted that the Egyptians will be unable to drink its water.'"

Moses and Aaron carried out God's command, and the water in rivers, streams, pools, wells and water jars became bloody.

This was the first plague.

But Pharao did not give in.

A second plague came. The Nile became filled with frogs, which came swarming up its banks to invade the land — streets, public squares, homes and even beds!

The third plague occurred when Aaron struck the dust of the earth, which turned into great swarms of winged insects that made life miserable for both men and animals.

Then there were the flies that infested everything. This was the fourth plague. This was followed by the death of many of the horses, cattle, camels, donkeys and sheep of the Egyptians. This was the fifth plague.

Then Moses took two handfuls of soot from a furnace and flung it into the air. The dust blew far and wide, causing painful boils to rise on the skin of men and the hides of beasts. But Pharao did not give in even in the face of this sixth plague. Then the sky filled with clouds; there were great peals of thunder and flashes of lightning, and a fierce hail poured down upon the land—the seventh plague.

This was followed by an invasion of locusts, which devoured everything that remained after the hail storm. This was the eighth plague, and Pharao was really shaken by it. As he had done a few times before, he promised to let the people go, but then as soon as the danger had passed he took back his promise.

Then a great darkness fell over the land of Egypt for three days. After it had gone, Moses and Aaron went to have a discussion with Pharao. But Pharao still refused to give in.

The reason Pharao was so stubborn, was that the Egyptians were accustomed to seeing some of these things happen. Every year, at the beginning of the spring floods, the Nile turned red because of great quantities of volcanic ash picked up by the high waters; at other times, frogs swarmed up the riverbanks and overran the countryside; so, too, the scorching winds from the nearby desert often picked up so much sand in the springtime as to blot out the light of the sun.

But this time it was God who had brought about these disturbing things. These were true miracles worked by him; in fact, they took place one after another, and when Moses gave the signal, rather than at different seasons, and only the Egyptians were bothered by them, while the Israelites were not.

In God's name, Moses and Aaron now threatened Pharao with the tenth plague, the worst of all: the death of all the first-born children of the Egyptians. Pharao still stubbornly refused to let the Hebrews go.

God ordered Moses and Aaron to prepare the people for flight.

"Tell the whole community of Israel," God said to Moses, "that every family must obtain for itself a lamb without blemish, and then kill it during the evening twilight. They shall take some of its blood and apply it to the two doorposts and to the lintel of the house. That same night they shall eat its roasted flesh with unleavened bread and bitter herbs. They must eat it with sandals on their feet and their staffs in their hands, like those who are in flight. For I will go through Egypt and strike down every first-born of the land except in the houses where there is the blood of the lamb"

All the Israelite families did as Moses commanded.

And then an angel of death killed all the first-born sons of the Egyptians, including the son of Pharao. But the angel passed over every home which had the lamb's blood on its doorposts. For that reason, the paschal lamb whose blood saved the Hebrews is now seen to be a type or symbol of Christ, the Lamb of God, whose death saved us all from slavery to sin.

Hearing the loud wailing of the Egyptians, the Pharao called Moses and Aaron. He ordered them to leave with all the Israelites at once to offer sacrifice to the Lord in the desert.

Thus, after many years in Egypt, the Hebrew people left for the Promised Land. This journey is called the Exodus. It is also called the Passover, from which comes our English word *paschal*, referring to the celebration of the Jewish Passover and the Christian Easter.

"This day," the Lord had told the Israelites, "shall be a memorial feast for you, which all your generations shall celebrate with lasting ceremony"

And indeed, in the desert and in the Promised Land of Chanaan the Israelites would never forget to celebrate the Passover feast. It was the duty of the youngest son in the family to ask his father the reason for the ceremony. Every year the father would repeat the same explanation: "This is the Passover sacrifice of the Lord, who, when we were slaves of the Egyptians, passed over the houses of the Israelites while he struck down the Egyptians. He set us free...."

The Israelites set out for the Promised Land. God, who is all-powerful, saw to it that they crossed the Red Sea miraculously. He sent a strong, hot wind from the east, which blew for several hours and drove the waters off a shallow crossing place. The Israelites crossed on dry land. Then God let the wind stop, and the waters flowed back to their usual position. These waters caught the Egyptians, who had changed their minds and were chasing the Israelites. The Bible recounts the miracle in these words:

Then Moses stretched out his hand over the sea, and the Lord swept the sea with a strong east wind all night long and so turned it into dry land. When the water was thus divided, the Israelites marched into the midst of the sea on dry land, with the water like a wall to their right and to their left. The Egyptians followed in pursuit; all Pharao's horses and chariots and charioteers went after them right into the midst of the sea.... Then the Lord told Moses: "Stretch out your hand over the sea, that the water may flow back upon the Egyptians, upon their chariots and their charioteers." So Moses stretched out his hand over the sea, and at dawn the sea flowed back to its normal depth. As the water flowed back, it covered the chariots and the charioteers of Pharao's whole army which had followed the Israelites into the sea.

The passage through the Red Sea is a symbol or type of baptism, by which we are freed from the slavery to sin, as the Hebrews were freed from their slavery to Pharao.

From the Red Sea the Hebrews began to travel through the desert of the Sinai peninsula. God went ahead of them as a bright cloud by day and a fiery cloud by night. But the Israelites began to complain. When their food ran out in the desert, they began to long for the meat and tasty food they had had in Egypt.

Moses then told them, "The Lord will give you meat to eat this evening and tomorrow he will give you your fill of bread."

In the evening a flock of tasty birds called quail appeared and covered the camp. The Hebrews took them and ate their fill.

In the morning, when they arose, they found fine white flakes on the ground. They went about asking each other: "Manu?" – which in their language meant: "What is this?" Thus the food was called *manna*. The manna fell every morning, except on Saturday, which was the Sabbath. It tasted like wafers made with honey. Everyone was to gather enough manna for the day, and on the day before Saturday all gathered a double amount.

The manna came down six days a week, year in and year out, for forty years, until the Israelites entered the Promised Land.

Manna was a symbol of the Holy Eucharist, the true Bread of Heaven, which sustains us in the desert of life.

When the water supply ran out, Moses struck a rock in the presence of the people, by command of God, and at once a

great supply of fresh water gushed forth to satisfy the Hebrews' thirst.

Should we envy the Israelites because of all the things God did for them in the desert? Not at all! God lovingly provides for our *spiritual* needs in an even more marvelous manner. He sent his own Son, our Lord Jesus Christ, to save us. Jesus Christ lives in our midst, in the Blessed Sacrament of the altar. He is the food of our souls in Holy Communion. He forgives our sins in confession. God has given each of us a guardian angel, too. The Lord gives to all men the graces they need to save their souls. (If they are not saved, it is their own fault.)

In the third month after their departure from Egypt, the Hebrews reached the foot of Mount Sinai.

Moses went up the mountain and received from God the following order: "On the third day the Lord will come down on Mount Sinai before the eyes of all the people. Set limits for the people all around the mountain and tell them: Take care not to go up the mountain, or even to touch its base."

On the morning of the third day there were bursts of thunder and lightning, and a heavy cloud over the mountain, and a very loud trumpet blast, so that all the people in the camp trembled.

Moses led the people out of the camp to meet God. Fearfully, they stationed themselves at the foot of the mountain. Alone, Moses went up. Then from the top of the mountain, God said:

"I, the Lord, am your God.

"You shall not have other gods besides me, nor shall you worship them. For I, the Lord your God, am a jealous God, punishing those who hate me, but showing mercy to those who love me and keep my commandments.

"You shall not take the name of the Lord, your God, in vain.

"Remember to keep holy the Sabbath Day. Six days you may labor, but on the seventh, no work may be done.

"Honor your father and your mother, that you may have a long life.

"You shall not kill.

"You shall not commit impure acts.

"You shall not steal.

"You shall not bear false witness against your neighbor.

"You shall not covet your neighbor's wife.

"You shall not covet your neighbor's house or any other thing that belongs to him."

All the people solemnly promised to obey these Ten Commandments of the Lord. "We will do everything that the Lord has told us!" they exclaimed.

God gave these very same commandments to us, too, for we are the New People of God. It is our duty to know and practice them. By keeping the Ten Commandments, we show our love of God and neighbor and live a good and happy life.

Moses stayed on the mountain forty days and forty nights. During that time, the Lord gave him many other commands.

But down below, the people grew tired of waiting for Moses. They gathered around Aaron and said to him, "Come, make us a god who will be our leader; as for Moses, we do not know what has happened to him."

Aaron had them bring their golden earrings to him and, fashioning this gold with an engraving tool, he made a calf of gold as a pagan would do. He built an altar and invited the people to adore the new god. The Israelites made a great feast for the golden calf, adored it and offered sacrifices.

Meanwhile, the Lord had given Moses two stone tablets on which he had carved the Ten Commandments.

When Moses came down the mountain and saw the golden calf and the dancing, his anger sprang up and rightfully so. He threw the tablets down and broke them on the base of the mountain. He melted the calf in the fire and severely punished everyone who had adored it as a god. Then he went up the mountain again and asked pardon of the Lord for his people's sin.

Forty days later he returned with two tablets like the first, upon which the Ten Commandments were carved. His face glowed with light.

On the mountain God had told Moses: "The sons of Israel must build me a sanctuary, for I wish to dwell in their midst."

Moses called the best craftsmen among the Israelites and had them build the Tabernacle, or Dwelling, according to the directions God had given him.

The Dwelling was a splendid and marvelous sight. Its walls were of wood, and its roof of beautifully-woven mats. Inside, it was divided into two parts: the Holy Place and the Holy of Holies.

The Holy Place contained the altar of incense, upon which the priests were to burn sweet-smelling substances in honor of God.

The Holy of Holies contained the Ark of the Covenant, a gold-plated chest holding the tablets of the Commandments which God had given to Moses. On the Ark rested a flat piece of gold, upon which knelt two golden statues of angels.

The Lord also told Moses: "From among the Israelites have your brother Aaron, together with his sons...brought to you, that they may be my priests." Moses had splendid vestments made, as God directed, and consecrated Aaron as high priest. Aaron's sons were also consecrated priests; other members of their tribe, the levites, became their helpers. The priests were to offer God sacrifices and incense.

The altar of burned offerings, or holocausts, was in the enclosure that surrounded the Dwelling; there animals were burned as sacrifices. The altar was large and square. It was wooden and shaped like a hollow box that could be carried from one place to another by means of poles slipped through rings in its corners.

Between the altar and the Dwelling stood the laver, an enormous bronze bowl standing upon a bronze base. Before entering the Dwelling, the priests were to draw water from the laver in order to wash their hands and feet.

The Dwelling, laver and altar of holocausts stood in a court surrounded by a wall formed of bronze pedestals and columns, between which linen draperies were hung.

When the Dwelling had been completed, a cloud came down and covered it, thus showing the sons of Israel that God was in their midst. Every time that the cloud rose up from the Dwelling, the Israelites would take down the enclosure, the Dwelling, and their own tents and follow the cloud as it moved on ahead of them. They carried the Ark by means of gold-plated poles slipped through golden rings attached to its sides.

The Israelites marched or pitched camp only when and where God commanded them to do so. They were under his protection. The Lord had chosen to live in their midst, and he was leading them visibly; they thus saw that he was keeping the covenant he had made with them on Mount Sinai. The sacrifices which their priests were to offer for all of them, were to be a sign of the people's gratitude to God and their loyalty to him.

As the travels of the Hebrews in the desert continued, Moses sent explorers into the land which God had promised to them. The explorers returned carrying a large cluster of grapes and some figs and other fruits, larger than they had ever seen before. However, most of these men were afraid of the Chanaanites, so they told Moses that the Hebrews would surely be killed if they tried to enter the Promised Land.

70

Notwithstanding the many miracles worked by God for his people, they often distrusted him and complained against Moses. For this, the Lord punished them: "Of all the men who have seen my glory and the signs I worked in Egypt," he said, "not one shall see the land which I promised on oath to their fathers. They will all die in the desert and their children under twenty will enter the Promised Land."

After the Hebrews had wandered in the desert for forty years in punishment for their sins, God revealed to Moses that he would soon die. He told Moses to choose Josue, a good man and a good fighter, to take his place. Then the great leader blessed the twelve tribes of Israel one by one and breathed forth his soul to God.

Rejoice, O hearts that seek the Lord;
glory in his holy name.
He sent Moses his servant,
Aaron, whom he had chosen.
They worked his signs in Egypt,
and he led them forth.
He spread a cloud to cover them
and fire to give them light by night.
They asked, and he brought them quail,
and with bread from heaven he satisfied them.
And he led forth his people with joy,
with shouts of joy, his chosen ones.

Psalm 104

Josue

After Moses' death, the Spirit of God descended upon Josue. The Lord told him, "Prepare to cross the Jordan here, with all the people, into the land I will give the Israelites. I will be with you as I was with Moses. Be firm and faithful, taking care to observe the entire Law which my servant Moses commanded you. Be firm and faithful! Do not fear nor be discouraged, for the Lord your God is with you wherever you go."

Well understanding his mission, Josue bravely shouldered his responsibility. The future of his people depended upon him.

Calling the leaders of the Israelites, he ordered them to go through their camp and tell the people: "Prepare food and gather up your belongings, for three days from now you will cross the River Jordan at the nearest place, to march in and take possession of the land which the Lord, your God, is giving you."

After three days of excited preparation, the march to the riverbank began. This was such an important event for the Hebrews—who were finally entering the Promised Land after their long exile in Egypt and forty years in the desert!—that they formed into a solemn procession. The Ark was sent on ahead of them, for it contained the Ten Commandments and was to remind the Hebrews that they had to let God's Law guide them in all that they did.

The priests carrying the Ark reached the river and waded into it at a crossing place. Because of winter rains and melting snows, the waters were much deeper than usual; yet as soon as the priests stepped into the Jordan, the waters flowing down from upstream halted, while those flowing downstream toward the Dead Sea disappeared entirely.

Then, the people crossed over opposite the city of Jericho, walking right through the riverbed. While they crossed, the priests carrying the Ark of the Covenant stood still in the bed of the Jordan. Then, when the entire Hebrew nation had crossed, they, too, set foot on the Promised Land, and the Jordan waters again came flowing by.

It is not impossible that the river waters had been held back by some natural cause. Earthquakes and landslides are common in the Jordan valley, and the river's waters were blocked by them in 1267 and 1927. But the Book of Josue tells us that no matter how the waters were blocked, it was a miracle worked by God, because God caused it to happen at the right moment—and it was still more marvelous because the river was very high at that season. God is love, and he can very well work whatever miracles he wishes for those whom he loves.

That day God made Josue great in the eyes of all the people of Israel and from then on, throughout his entire life, they respected him as they had respected Moses.

Josue and the Israelites now found themselves before Jericho, the city which blocked their path, for it was truly the gateway into the Promised Land.

Now Jericho was strongly barred because of the presence of the Israelites, and no one left it or entered it. But the Lord said to Josue, "I have given Jericho and its king into your power. Have all the soldiers circle the city, marching once around it. Do this each day for six days, with seven priests carrying rams' horns marching ahead of the Ark. On the seventh day march around the city seven times, and have the priests blow the horns. When they give a long blast, that is your signal. Let all the people shout aloud. The wall of the city will collapse, and your people will be able to attack the city."

Josue had this command of the Lord carried out exactly. Once a day for seven days the procession marched around the walls of Jericho, the perimeter of which was about 2,660 feet. On the seventh day they circled the city seven times. At the blowing of the rams' horns, the Israelites let out a ringing war cry. The walls of the city collapsed, and the people rushed in to conquer it.

Scientists called archaeologists, who have found and studied the old walls of Jericho, tell us that they fell outward at various points.

Certainly it is easy to see the hand of God's providence in the collapse of the walls, for in the land of the warlike Chanaanites a defeat in their first battle would have put an end to all the Israelites' hopes and dreams.

By means of Josue God had led his people into the land he had promised to the patriarchs, Abraham, Isaac and Jacob.

But there were many peoples living in Chanaan who were stronger and more powerful than the Hebrews.

God, however, is stronger than anyone else and the ruler of the earth; he granted his people victory over all their enemies. One after another the strongholds and fortified cities fell into their hands. Soon they had established themselves throughout the land. Thus did God keep the promise he had made to his people, and thus did Josue win the Lord's holy war and preserve the people God had chosen to be his own.

Right to the end, Josue was a faithful servant of the Lord, working to make him loved. In the spiritual testament he left his people, he said several things which are good for us, too: "You must remain loyal to the Lord your God as you have been to this day.... Fear the Lord and serve him with sincerity and loyalty."

With one voice, all the people answered, "We will serve the Lord our God and obey his commandments."

Give thanks to the Lord, for he is good,
for his mercy endures forever.
He alone does great wonders;
he made the heavens in wisdom.
He led his people through the desert,
and smote great kings,
and slew powerful kings.
He made their land a heritage,
the heritage of Israel his servant.
Give thanks to the God of heaven,
for his mercy endures forever.
Psalm 135

The Judges
and the First King

Now in possession of the Promised Land, the Israelites lived happily and peacefully—as long as they worshiped God and kept his commandments.

But after the death of Josue and everyone else who had seen the great wonders that God had done for his people, the Israelites forgot the Lord and the covenant they had made with him, and began to worship the idols of the Chanaanites—those pagan peoples who still lived in their midst. The Chanaanite religion was very easy to practice.

Whenever the Israelites turned away from the law of God and from his love, he recalled them to their senses, even permitting them to be punished by pagan conquests. God is not only merciful but also just. Each of these punishments lasted until the Israelites became sorry for their sins and prayed for help from the Lord.

Little by little, they would learn that no one can be happy without God. Leaving him always brings about misery and confusion. Life loses its peace and becomes a struggle.

Every time his people turned to him, God freed them from their pagan conquerors by choosing some Israelite with special qualities of goodness, wisdom and justice to be his representative. This man or woman was called a judge. The word "judge" meant "liberator" or "savior."

With divine help, each judge freed the Israelites from the enemies who had invaded their land, bringing death and destruction. The Lord was with each of the judges until death.

Among these leaders were: Debora, Gedeon, Jephte, Samson and Samuel.

The judges were not kings. The king of the Israelites was the Lord—no one else. But the people wished to have a king like all the nations around them, so they said to Samuel, the last of the judges, who was now very old, "Make us a king, to judge us, as all nations have."

The Lord heard the request of his people and said to Samuel, "Listen to their voice and make them a king."

Inspired by God, Samuel anointed Saul as the king. Saul was tall and strong, the bravest of all the fighting men of Israel. Samuel told the Israelites, "Surely you see that there is no one among all the people like him whom the Lord has chosen."

And all the people cried out, "God save the king!"

The king of Israel was not to be like the kings of other nations, which were pagan. Instead, he was to be the representative of God and the ruler of the people according to God's will. As long as Saul obeyed God's laws faithfully, he was blessed, and won great victories over his enemies; but then he grew proud and sinned. He disobeyed Samuel. God was greatly displeased by this.

Therefore, the Lord chose another leader for his people, a king after his own heart—David!

You are my God; have pity on me, O Lord,
for to you I call all the day.
For you, O Lord, are good and forgiving,
abounding in kindness to all who call upon you.
Psalm 85

David and Solomon

"Fill your horn with oil," God said to Samuel, "and go to Bethlehem, to the house of Jesse, for I have provided a king from among his sons."

Samuel went to Bethlehem and Jesse presented his sons to him, one by one, but none of them was the one whom God had chosen.

"Are all your sons here?" the prophet asked Jesse.

"No," Jesse replied. "There is still the youngest one, who is watching the sheep."

"Send for him."

When the boy David was brought in, Samuel took the oil in his horn and poured it on the boy's head, consecrating him king of Israel in the name of the Lord. As soon as Samuel had done this, the Spirit of God departed from Saul and came upon David. But Saul did not know that the boy David was now king.

Some time later, Saul was fighting the Philistines, who were trying to take over the land of Israel. The two armies camped on mountains facing each other, with a valley between them. They remained this way for many days. Then the Philistine giant, Goliath, stepped forward. About ten feet tall, completely covered with armor, he dared the Israelites to fight him. "Choose a man from among you," he challenged, "and let him come down and fight hand to hand. If he kills me, we will be your servants, but if I kill him, you shall serve us." '

No Hebrew had yet dared to accept the challenge, when young David appeared on the scene. As soon as the boy saw the giant, he asked, "Who is this Philistine that he should challenge the armies of the living God?"

Someone told King Saul what David had said, and Saul sent for him. When he was brought in before the king, David said, "Let no one be afraid. I your servant will go to fight the Philistine."

At first Saul protested that David was too young, but then he let him go. The boy took up his shepherd's staff and picked five smooth stones out of a brook. These he put into a pouch and then, taking a sling in his hand, he calmly walked toward the Philistine.

Goliath came on. When he was but a short distance from David, he cried out, "Am I a dog, that you come to me with a staff? Come ahead, and I will give your flesh to the birds and beasts to eat."

"You come to me with a sword, a spear and a shield," replied David, "but I come to you in the name of the Lord of hosts, the God of the armies of Israel, which you have challenged. The Lord will deliver you to me and I will kill you. Everyone who is here will know that God saves without a sword or a spear. This is his battle, and he will deliver you into our hands."

As the Philistine came on, David quickly put his hand into his pouch, took a stone and placed it in his sling, and whirled the sling around his head. The stone flew swiftly through the air and struck Goliath on the forehead. The giant fell to the ground. He had been knocked out. David ran up to him, took up the giant's own great sword and cut off his head with it.

Seeing their champion dead, the Philistines fled, but the Israelites chased them and killed many of them. Saul was overjoyed at the victory. He sent for David and took him to his palace. Then he made him a captain in his army. David became a great soldier and led Saul's fighting men to many victories against the Philistines.

But when David returned to the palace after his great victories, the Hebrew women came out to meet him, playing musical instruments and singing for joy—praising Saul, but praising David still more. "Saul killed his thousands," they sang, "and David his ten thousands." And right away, Saul became jealous.

Jealousy can have very bad effects. Saul began to be afraid that David would take over his kingdom. The people loved and praised David more and more. And Saul grew more and more jealous. He told his sons and his servants that he wanted David to be killed.

See how far Saul's jealousy took him? Man is able to do evil. God will not stop him, as he did not stop Adam and Eve or Cain or Saul. But unhappy is he who does evil!

Learning of Saul's plans, David fled to the mountains, where many good Hebrew fighting men joined him.

Meanwhile the war with the Philistines continued. On the mountains of Gelboe, the Hebrew army was overcome and put to flight. Many were killed, and Saul, in despair, threw himself on his own sword and died.

David wept bitterly for Saul, although the king had made him suffer very much. He even composed a funeral hymn in Saul's honor and punished everyone who spoke badly of him.

Now all the people came to David in Hebron and proclaimed him king. And he and his fighting men went over to Jerusalem, a city which was still in the hands of the pagans. Because of Jerusalem's high, strong walls, the Israelites had never been able to conquer it. King David and his men captured the city and made it the capital of all the land.

One of David's first cares was the building of a beautiful tabernacle in which to place the holy Ark of the Covenant. He built it on Mt. Sion, the highest point in the city of Jerusalem. The Ark was brought into the city with very great solemnity.

Holy King David ruled over Israel for forty years, and the Lord blessed the whole land and extended the boundaries of the kingdom. Yet, David did not have a peaceful rule. Challenged by Saul's sons, and attacked by neighboring tribes, he was forced to fight continually. However, he was always victorious.

David was a real hero, a man after God's own heart. Success did not make him proud, and in trouble he always trusted God and accepted his will. Whenever he had to decide something, he prayed to learn God's will. The honor and worship of God were his chief concern.

He had a wonderful gift of poetry, which he used in writing beautiful prayers to the Lord, called psalms. A great prophet also, David sang the praises of the Messia who would be his descendant. This blood relationship with the Savior of the world is the holy king's greatest glory.

In spite of all this David, too, sinned. God sent the prophet Nathan to speak the following parable to him: "There were two men in a city, the one rich and the other poor. The rich man had a great many sheep and oxen. But the poor man had nothing but a little lamb which had grown up in his house together with his children, eating his bread, drinking from his cup, and sleeping on his bosom. It was like a daughter to him. One day a certain stranger came to the rich man. In order to make a feast for the stranger, the rich man did not take his own sheep and oxen, but he took the poor man's lamb."

Angered at such injustice, David cried out, "As the Lord lives, the one who did this is worthy of death! He should give back four lambs in reparation for having acted so cruelly!"

Then Nathan said to David, "You are that man! Thus says the Lord God of Israel: I anointed you king over Israel, I delivered you from Saul's hand, I gave you his palace and the house of Israel and Juda. If these things be little, I shall add far greater things. Why, therefore, have you disobeyed the word of the Lord, to do evil in my sight?... In punishment, I will raise up evil against you, the sword shall never depart from your house and you shall have much to suffer!"

David exclaimed, "I have sinned against the Lord!" He wept bitterly over the evil he had done and wrote Psalm 50, the *Miserere*, the most beautiful psalm of sorrow for personal sin.

In the name of God, Nathan told David that the Lord had forgiven him for his sin, but that he would have to do great penance. So it was. On that very day, a child of David's died and later on, Absalom, his first-born son, whom he greatly loved, rebelled against him. Grief-stricken, David had to leave his palace, and Absalom took it for himself. Then Absalom was forced to flee from the palace, however, for David's followers chased him. While riding through a forest, Absalom's long hair caught in the branches of a tree and one of David's men killed him, in spite of David's command not to do so. Over and over again, the king had said: "Save me the boy Absalom." David wept much over his son's death.

When he returned to Jerusalem, it was amid the loud shouts of welcome of his people, by whom he was greatly loved.

When he reached the age of seventy and felt that death was near, holy David had his son Solomon consecrated king, praying that the Lord would give him a glorious reign. Calling his son to himself, he said, "Solomon, my son, I am about to die. Take courage and show yourself a man. Obey the Lord your God, walking in his ways, observing his ceremonies and precepts and judgments and testimonies as it is written in the law of Moses..."

Solomon was recognized and applauded by all the people, and his reign—from 961 B.C. to 925 B.C.—was peaceful and glorious, as no other king of Israel's had been.

After he had ascended to the throne, the Lord told him, "Ask what you will and I shall give it to you."

Solomon asked for wisdom and understanding in order to judge God's people worthily.

God was pleased at Solomon's request and He answered, "Because you have asked this and have not asked for a long life or riches or glory but have asked for yourself wisdom to understand judgment, behold, I have done as you asked. I have given you such a wise and understanding heart that there has never been anyone like you, nor will there ever be. Besides this, I also give you those things for which you did not ask: riches and glory, so that no one has been like you before nor will be."

Solomon governed Israel and Juda for thirty-eight years. During this period, there was great peace and prosperity.

The fame of Solomon's wealth and his marvelous wisdom reached even to the most distant kingdoms, and Egyptian and Oriental kings came to see him.

Solomon spoke many parables, or maxims; he composed many songs.

Solomon's greatest work, however, was the building of the magnificent Temple of Jerusalem.

He had rich materials brought to Jerusalem from every part of the world. He called highly experienced foreign laborers and employed one hundred and sixty thousand workers, watched over by three thousand foremen.

The Temple was encircled by wide porches, with decorated columns. In the middle was built the sanctuary, which was reserved to the priests. At its center was the Holy of Holies, which could be entered only once a year by the high priest. The walls, the sanctuary and the cherubs who spread their wings over the holy Ark, were covered with finely worked gold.

When, after seven and a half years, the work on the Temple was finished, Solomon called the people of Israel to the solemn dedication. The Ark of the Covenant was solemnly brought from Mt. Sion to the new Temple.

On that occasion, twenty-two thousand oxen and one hundred twenty thousand sheep were sacrificed. The feast lasted fourteen days.

Solomon also built a palace for himself, the like of which had never before been seen. Everywhere there was magnificence in gold, silver, emeralds and diamonds — all of unimaginable value. Solomon saw to it that all goods were distributed equally. His servants worked in a very orderly fashion so that everything went along exactly as it should.

When the Queen of Saba came to see Solomon, she was so struck with wonder that she exclaimed, "Blessed are your men and blessed are your servants who stand before you always and hear your wisdom! Blessed be the Lord, your God, who was pleased to set you upon the throne."

Yet, even Solomon sinned. In the later years of his life, he let himself be fooled by foreign princesses. He built temples for them, and so as not to displease them, he even worshiped pagan gods and burnt incense in their honor. The Lord therefore told him: "Because you have done this, and have not kept my covenant and my precepts which I have commanded you, I will divide and rend your kingdom.... I will rend it out of the hand of your son"

And so it came about. After Solomon's death the great kingdom was split into two parts—Israel to the north and Juda to the south. All the kings of Israel and most of the kings of Juda broke the covenant which their ancestors had made with the Lord. The people, too, turned away from God and again worshiped the idols of the pagans. Wars broke out again, and the glory of the Hebrew nation began to fade.

Have mercy on me, O God, in your goodness;
in the greatness of your compassion wipe out my offense.
Thoroughly wash me from my guilt
and of my sin cleanse me.
For I admit my offense,
and my sin if before me always.
A clean heart create for me, O God,
and a steadfast spirit renew in me.
My sacrifice, O God, is a contrite spirit;
a heart sorrowful and humbled, O God, you will not reject.

Psalm 50

The Prophets and the Exile

Even though the people were not faithful to God, he remained faithful to them. He sent them the prophets, good and upright men filled with the Holy Spirit. Under God's inspiration, they *scolded* the kings and the people for abandoning the ways of God; they *threatened* punishments, which always came about unless the people did penance; they *explained* the law of Moses and *consoled* the people with the hope of a future Messia, of whom they painted a beautiful picture in words.

Many centuries before the birth of Jesus Christ, the prophets had described the life of the Redeemer. In fact, they had spoken of his birthplace, of the adoration of the Magi, of the slaughter of the Holy Innocents, of the flight into Egypt and of the home of Jesus at Nazareth. The prophets spoke of the beginning of our Lord's preaching, of his miracles and of his titles of Master, God, Priest, Judge.... They described his passion and death, his resurrection and his ascension into heaven; they foretold his greatness and the spread of his Church throughout the world.

One of the great prophets was Elia. He presented himself before King Achab of Israel, who worshiped the pagan god Baal. "Send for all Israel to meet me at Mount Carmel," said Elia, "together with four hundred and fifty prophets of Baal"

Achab sent for the people and the prophets, and they gathered on Mount Carmel. Elia invited the prophets of the false god to kill a bull and place it on an altar. He himself would do the same. "Call upon the names of your gods," he said, "and I will call upon the name of my Lord; and the God that shall answer by fire will truly be God." And all the people agreed to this.

Elia gave the prophets of Baal the first try. They made an altar and laid their bull on it. Then all morning long they called upon Baal to send down fire from heaven, but nothing happened.

Now it was Elia's turn. Taking twelve stones in memory of the twelve tribes of Israel, he made an altar upon which he placed wood and the bull for the sacrifice. Then he ordered several buckets of water to be poured on the victim and the wood. When everything had been thoroughly soaked, he stood before the altar and prayed: "O Lord God of Abraham, and Isaac and Israel, show this day that you are the God of Israel and that I am your servant, and that according to your commandment I have done all these things. Hear me, O Lord, hear me, that this people may learn that you are the Lord God."

Then the fire of the Lord fell, and burned up the holocaust, the wood, and the very stones. And when all the people saw this, they fell on their faces and said, "The Lord is God, the Lord is God"

But the Israelites were quick to forget the miracle of the fire from heaven. The rulers of the northern kingdom continued in their wicked ways, until 722 B.C., when the Assyrians invaded the land and took the people of Israel off to their country as prisoners. Then the king of Assyria brought pagans into that part of the Promised Land and had a priest of the Lord teach them how to worship God. But when these people worshiped the Lord, they served also their own gods according to the customs of the nations out of which they were brought.

The people of Juda were more faithful to God, especially during the reign of good King Ezechia. At that time a great prophet named Isaia lived in Juda. Besides warning the people to be true to the Lord, he foretold the exile of the kingdom of Juda into Babylon. This is what he wrote: "Hear, O heavens, and give ear, O earth, for the Lord has spoken. I have brought up children and exalted them, but they have despised me. They have forsaken the Lord; they have blasphemed the Holy One of Israel, they are gone away backwards.... For this reason, their land shall be desolate, their cities burnt with fire, and their possessions devoured by strangers. The daughter of Sion (that is, Jerusalem) shall be as a city laid waste" (see Isaia 1).

However, Isaia also foretold the return of the exiled Jews to their homeland, the rebuilding of the Temple of Jerusalem which had been destroyed by the Babylonians. He spoke of the virginity of the Mother of God, of the life, passion and death of our Savior, and of the glory of the Church.

The man of sorrows, the prophet Jeremia, also foretold the ruin of Jerusalem and of his country, and prophesied that the Hebrews would be captives in Babylon for seventy years.

In fact, during the prophet's very lifetime, the powerful emperor of Babylon, Nabuchadonosor, invaded Juda and took over Jerusalem. He carried away everything precious from the royal palace and the Temple of the Lord. Then he burned the city and took all its people and its king away into Babylon. The year was 587 B.C. This was the beginning of the Babylonian Exile.

Jeremia himself remained amidst the ruins of Jerusalem, but later some of his countrymen forced him to go down to Egypt with them, where he died.

The Hebrews in Babylon had a long time to reflect upon the justice of the Lord and their own guilt. The Book of the prophet Daniel records some of their feelings:

> Great and awesome God....
> We have rebelled
> and departed from your commandments
> and your laws.
> We have not obeyed your servants the prophets,
> who spoke in your name
> to our kings, our princes, our fathers,
> and all the people of the land.
> Justice, O Lord, is on your side....
> We have sinned, we are guilty....
> O Lord, hear! O Lord, pardon!

Through the prophet Ezechiel, the Lord gave hope to the Hebrew exiles in Babylon:

> As a shepherd tends his flock...
> so will I tend my sheep....
> I will gather them from the foreign lands;
> I will bring them back to their own country
> and pasture them upon the mountains of Israel.

When Cyrus the king of the Persians conquered Babylon, he set the Hebrews free and let them return to their homeland, which would no longer be an independent kingdom but a part of the Persian Empire. Among those who returned to Jerusalem were Zorobabel, a descendant of the royal family of Juda, who together with the priest Josue supervised the rebuilding of the Temple; Nehemia, who took charge of rebuilding the ruined walls of the city; and a holy priest named Ezra. The prophet Zacharia foretold the entrance of the Messia into the restored city:

> Rejoice heartily, O daughter Sion!
> Shout for joy, O daughter Jerusalem!
> See, your king shall come to you.
> A just savior is he,
> meek, and riding on a donkey —
> on a colt, the foal of a donkey....
> His dominion shall be from sea to sea,
> and from the River
> to the ends of the earth.

One of the last prophets was Malachia. He foretold that a clean victim would be offered to God in every part of the earth. That prophecy is realized in the Holy Mass, which is offered in every part of the world. Malachia also promised that a Precursor of the Messia would appear. This would be St. John the Baptist.

Sing to the Lord a new song,
for he has done wondrous deeds.
All the ends of the earth have seen
the salvation by our God.
Let the sea and what fills it resound,
the mountains shout with them for joy
Before the Lord, for he comes,
for he comes to rule the earth.

Psalm 97

The Coming of the Savior

The time foretold by the prophets had arrived. The sceptre of Juda had passed into the hands of a foreigner, Herod. The seventy weeks of years which the prophet Daniel had foretold were nearly over. The *peace* which was to reign over the earth at the birth of the Messia had been proclaimed by Caesar Augustus, the Roman Emperor. All nations, even pagan, sighed for and awaited a Savior. And the Savior came. Several months before him, however, was born the Precursor, St. John the Baptist.

Listen to the Gospel story itself:

In the time of Herod, king of Judea, there lived a husband and wife who were just and God-fearing. They kept the Commandments of God perfectly, but they were sad, because they had no children. The names of this holy couple were *Zachary* and *Elizabeth.*

Zachary was a priest, and his turn came to enter the Sanctuary of the Lord to offer incense. As he was incensing the altar, an angel appeared to him. Zachary was so frightened that he could not say a word.

"Do not be afraid, Zachary," said the angel, "for your prayer has been heard. Soon you shall have a son whom you shall call John. You shall have joy and gladness and many will rejoice at his birth. He shall be great before the Lord and shall be filled with the Holy Spirit even from his birth. He shall lead a very strict life and shall convert many people. He shall prepare for the Lord a well-disposed people"

Several months later, the Archangel Gabriel was sent from God to a town of Galilee, called Nazareth, to a virgin betrothed to a man of the house of David. The virgin's name was Mary.

Having come to her, the angel said, "Hail, full of grace; the Lord is with you! Blessed are you among women!"

Mary was troubled at these words. Deeply humble as she was, she kept wondering what kind of greeting this might be. But the angel told her: "Do not be afraid, Mary, for you have found grace with God. Behold, you shall be the mother of a son, whom you shall call Jesus. He shall be great and shall be called the Son of the Most High. The Lord God will give him the throne of David his father. He shall be King over the house of Jacob forever, and of his kingdom there shall be no end."

Mary asked, "How shall this happen, since I do not know man?"

"The Holy Spirit shall come upon you," explained the angel, "and the power of the Most High shall overshadow you. Therefore, the Holy One to be born of you shall be called the *Son of God.*"

Mary then spoke these beautiful words: "Behold the handmaid of the Lord; be it done to me according to your word." At that moment, she became the Mother of God.

The Birth of Jesus

In Nazareth, the Blessed Virgin Mary was awaiting the birth of her divine Son, Jesus Christ. Then from Rome came news that Caesar Augustus, Emperor of Rome, had ordered a census to be taken of the whole Roman Empire. Since Palestine, too, was a part of this empire, every Hebrew had to register, each in the city of his ancestors.

Mary and Joseph were descendants of the family of King David, who was born at Bethlehem in Judea.

Obedient to the emperor, they traveled from Nazareth in Galilee to Bethlehem. It was a long, tiresome journey. When they wearily arrived, they were unable to find shelter, although they went from one inn to another.

Finally, they turned their steps toward one of the many stables outside the city—a cave or grotto where animals were sheltered in bad weather.

It was in such a lowly stable, nevertheless blessed, that the King of heaven and earth, the Savior of the world, was born. He was born in the middle of the night, when all was peaceful and quiet. Mary wrapped the Infant Jesus in swaddling clothes and laid him in a manger. No doubt, she thought longingly of the little crib at Nazareth which St. Joseph had so lovingly prepared for Jesus, but then she surely willingly accepted the plans of God.

Jesus was born in the still of the night, while all was peaceful and quiet. He was born in an era of great peace for all nations. The prophets had already said that he is *the Prince of peace* and that when he would be born, there would be great peace on earth.

The first to adore the Infant Jesus were the most holy Virgin and St. Joseph. Next came the shepherds.

On the hills surrounding Bethlehem, there were many shepherds watching their flocks out in the open fields. Suddenly a great light surrounded them and an angel from heaven appeared before their wondering eyes. The shepherds were struck with fear. But the angel comforted them, saying,

"Do not be afraid! For behold, I bring you good news of great joy which shall be to all the people. For today, in the town of David, a Savior has been born to you who is Christ the Lord. And this shall be a sign to you: you will find an infant wrapped in swaddling clothes and lying in a manger."

Suddenly, there was with the angel who was speaking, a multitude of the heavenly host, praising God and saying, "Glory to God in the highest and on earth peace to men of good will."

When the beautiful vision was over, the shepherds, beside themselves with joy, said to one another: "Let us go over to

Bethlehem right away to see this thing which the Lord has made known to us." They took gifts and hurried to the stable. There they found Mary and Joseph and the Infant lying in the manger. Full of faith, they adored the newly born Messia and offered their gifts. Then they went into the streets of Bethlehem to spread the good news.

Eight days after his birth, the Infant was circumcised and given the name *Jesus*, as the angel had told Mary.

A law of Moses stated that the firstborn son of every family had to be presented in the Temple forty days after his birth, to be offered to the Lord. Mary obeyed the Lord perfectly, and on the day prescribed she made the offering of a pair of doves, as Moses had ordered.

When the Holy Family entered the Temple of Jerusalem, a old man named *Simeon* met them. He was a just, pious man who was anxiously awaiting the Redemption. The Holy Spirit had promised him that he would not die without seeing the anointed one of the Lord. Given light from heaven, the holy old man recognized the Infant Jesus as the Messia, and taking him into his arms, he exclaimed, "Now do you dismiss your servant in peace, O Lord, because my eyes have seen the Savior." Then, turning to Mary, Simeon said, "A sword shall pierce your soul." What sword? The sword of sorrow, for, indeed, Mary would one day have to watch the crucifixion and death of her beloved Son.

There was also in the Temple a holy woman named Anna. She, too, recognized the Infant Jesus as the promised Messia; full of joy, she praised God and spoke of the Infant to all who were waiting anxiously for the coming of the Messia.

The Visit of the Magi

Some months after Jesus' birth, the Magi, or wise men, arrived in Jerusalem, and they asked the people who came running to them in wonderment: "Where is he that is born King of the Jews? For we have seen his star in the East and have come to worship him."

Proud, cruel King Herod was troubled, and so was all Jerusalem with him. Neither the king nor his courtiers nor the people knew about the birth of the Messia. Herod certainly was not awaiting his birth, for he feared that he might lose his throne. At any rate, should the Messia be born, he would find a way to kill him. He gathered together all the chief priests and elders of the people, and the doctors of the Law. He inquired of them where the Christ was to be born.

"According to the prophecies, he should be born in Bethlehem," they answered. "For thus it is written by the prophet, 'And you, Bethlehem, of the land of Juda, are by no means least among the princes of Juda; for from you shall come forth a leader who shall rule my people Israel.'"

Herod called the Magi. Pointing out the way to Bethlehem, he said, "Go and diligently seek the Child; when you have found him, bring me word that I, too, may go and worship him."

Without suspecting anything, the Magi promised and again started on their way toward Bethlehem, where they found the Child with his mother. Enlightened by grace, they recognized the Son of God in that Child and, falling to their knees, they worshiped him.

They had planned to return to Jerusalem the next day. But during the night an angel warned them in a dream not to return to Herod. They therefore went back to their own country by another way.

The Flight into Egypt

After the Magi left, the angel of the Lord appeared to Joseph in a dream and told him, "Rise, take the Child and his mother and flee into Egypt. Remain there until I tell you. For Herod will seek the Child to destroy him."

Promptly Joseph obeyed. He, Mary and the Infant started out for Egypt in the middle of the night.

When Herod realized that he had been tricked by the Magi, he flew into a rage and ordered all the baby boys, two years old or younger, of Bethlehem and its neighborhood to be killed. The cruel king thought that by doing that, he would also kill Jesus.

Having committed that great crime, King Herod had no peace. Horrible diseases struck his body, and he was continually tormented by a great thirst. He became unbearable, even to himself, until he finally drew his last breath.

After the murderous tyrant's death, the angel of the Lord appeared to Joseph in Egypt, in a dream. "Rise," he told him, "take the Boy and his mother and go into the land of Israel, because they who desired the death of the Child are dead."

The Holy Family set out at once. When they reached Palestine, they discovered that Herod's son, Archelaus, was reigning on his father's throne. Joseph was fearful, for he knew that Archelaus was just as cruel as his father had been. Then the angel warned him to go into Galilee, rather than to Judea, where Archelaus reigned. So Joseph retired to Nazareth, a little city hidden among the mountains. For this reason Jesus was called a Nazarene.

Finding in the Temple

Like any other boy, Jesus at Nazareth learned his father's trade; he became a carpenter. Jesus seemed no different from his companions, and no one even imagined that he was God.

At the age of twelve, a Hebrew boy became a "son of the Law," and it was on this occasion that Jesus showed a flash of his divinity. The Law commanded that all Hebrews were to go to the Temple in Jerusalem for the feast of the Passover. For a boy, this obligation began at the age of twelve. When Jesus reached that age, he went to the Temple in Jerusalem with St. Joseph and his mother. Nazareth was about eighty miles from Jerusalem and the trip was made on foot.

How good Jesus felt to be in the house of his Father! When the time came to leave the holy place, he felt he should remain. He had come into the world to make the light of truth shine forth, and he felt that his Father wanted him to show his holy mission.

Classes in the Temple were conducted by means of the question and answer method. In the midst of Hebrew teachers, Jesus immediately drew attention to himself because of his answers and the originality of his questions. The rabbis gathered about him and were greatly astonished at his wisdom. Who had taught him those very profound truths?

Jesus was God! He had come into the world to carry out his Father's business; that is, to establish the kingdom of God on earth.

After his parents came to find him, Jesus returned to Nazareth with them. There, in obedience and work, the Savior spent his hidden life, which lasted until he was about thirty years old.

Glory to God in the highest.
And on earth peace to men of good will.
We praise you. We bless you.
We worship you. We glorify you.
We give you thanks for your great glory.
Lord God, heavenly king, God the Father almighty.
Lord Jesus Christ, the only-begotten Son....
You alone, O Jesus Christ, are most high,
With the Holy Spirit, in the glory of God the Father.
Amen.

Jesus Begins His Public Life

The Baptism of Jesus

John, the son of Elizabeth and Zachary, was preaching on the banks of the Jordan. He wore a garment of camel's hair, and his food was locusts and wild honey. His eyes shone with God's light and his voice was strong and convincing.

John preached the baptism of repentance and the remission of sins.

"Repent, for the kingdom of heaven is at hand" (Matthew 3:2).

Crowds hurried to hear him preach and to be baptized by him in the Jordan. Many believed him to be the Messia, but John told them, "I am not the Messia."

The Jews from Jerusalem sent priests to ask him, "Who are you?"

"I am not the Christ," he replied.

"What, then? Are you the prophet Elia?"

"No."

"Who are you? What answer shall we give to those who sent us?"

"I am the voice of one crying in the desert, 'Make straight the way of the Lord!' as said Isaia the prophet."

"Why, then, do you baptize, if you are not the Christ, nor Elia, nor the prophet?"

"I baptize with water," answered John, "but in the midst of you has stood *One* whom you do not know. He it is who is to come after me, who has been set above me, the strap of whose sandal I am not worthy to loose. He will baptize you with the Holy Spirit and with fire."

While John was instructing and baptizing the people near the Jordan, Jesus left his house at Nazareth, by will of his Father, and presented himself to John to ask for baptism, too.

"What? Do you come to me?" John said to him, recognizing him to be the Messia. "It is I who ought to be baptized by you!"

But when Jesus insisted, John obeyed. And behold, immediately after Jesus was baptized, while he was still deep in prayer, the heavens opened, and the Holy Spirit in the form of a dove rested on his head, while a voice from the heavens said, "This is my beloved Son, in whom I am well pleased." It was the voice of the Father.

After his baptism, Jesus was led by the Spirit into the desert, where he fasted for forty days and forty nights. In the end, he was hungry. Then the devil came to tempt him, but he overcame the three temptations. When the devil left him, angels came to minister to him.

The Call of the Apostles

After fasting forty days in the desert, Jesus returned to the banks of the Jordan. As soon as John the Baptist saw him, he pointed Jesus out to his disciples and to the crowds around him, with these beautiful words, "Behold the Lamb of God, who takes away the sins of the world!" Every day in the Temple of Jerusalem, a lamb was offered to the Lord as a perpetual sacrifice. St. John called Jesus the Lamb of God who takes away the sins of the world, that is, the Messia who had come to sacrifice himself for the salvation of all men.

The next day John was with two of his disciples and seeing Jesus passing by, he said again, "Behold the Lamb of God!" Then the two disciples followed Jesus.

"What are you looking for?" the Lord asked the two men following him.

"Master, where do you live?"

"Come and see," Jesus replied.

The two men—Andrew, the brother of Simon, and John, the son of Zebedee—followed Jesus and stayed with him all day long. Then they returned home full of enthusiasm.

"Do you know!" said Andrew to his brother, "we have found the Messia." And he led him to Jesus. When Jesus saw Simon, he looked at him steadily for a moment and then said, "You are Simon, the son of John; you shall be called Peter." This means, *the rock.*

The next day, when Jesus was about to leave for Galilee, he met Philip and Nathanael and invited them to follow him.

Jesus later called other men to be his followers.

"Master," one said, "I will follow you wherever you go."

"The foxes have their dens and the birds of the air, their nests," answered Jesus, "but the Son of Man has no place to lay his head."

"Lord," another said to him, "first, let me go bury my father."

"Follow me," replied Jesus, "and let the dead bury their dead." With this answer, Jesus wanted to make the man understand that when God calls, we must answer at once.

A great crowd used to follow Jesus wherever he went. He felt sorry for them, because they were tired and disheartened, like sheep without a shepherd. He told his disciples, "The harvest is great, but the laborers are few. Pray, therefore, the Lord of the harvest to send good laborers into his harvest."

After preaching and working many miracles, Jesus dismissed the crowds and went up a mountain with His disciples to pray. He spent the whole night in prayer, and in the morning he chose twelve men from among his many followers. He called these twelve men *apostles,* which means *those sent forth.* They were: Simon, whom he called Peter, and Andrew his brother; James the Great and his brother John; Philip and Bartholomew; Thomas and Matthew; James the Less and

Thaddeus; Simon and finally, Judas Iscariot, who later betrayed Jesus.

To the twelve, our Lord gave power to cure the sick and cast out devils. They were his representatives, and upon them Jesus founded his Church.

Besides the apostles, Jesus chose seventy-two *disciples* and sent them two by two to preach the kingdom of God.

"Behold," he told them, "I send you forth as lambs in the midst of wolves; be prudent as serpents and simple as doves. He who hears you, hears me; he who despises you, despises me, and he who despises me, despises him who sent me."

"Lord," exclaimed the disciples, returning from preaching, "even the devils are subject to us in your name."

"I saw Satan falling as lightning from heaven," Jesus replied. "Yet do not rejoice that the spirits are subject to you. Rejoice rather that your names are written in heaven".

The Marriage Feast of Cana

When Jesus had just begun his public life, a wedding feast was held in Cana of Galilee. The Blessed Virgin Mary attended, and Jesus and his disciples were also invited. During the feast, the wine ran short. The Blessed Mother noticed it at once, and she said to Jesus, "They have no more wine."

"What would you have me do, woman?" replied Jesus. "My hour has not yet come."

It seemed a refusal. But the Blessed Mother did not give up. The hour for miracles had not yet come. With her faith, Mary hastened that hour. She called the servants and said to them, "Do whatever he tells you."

Near the banquet table were six stone water-jars. They were there because the Jews always washed their hands and their feet before eating. Each jar held a great deal of water.

Jesus said to the servants, "Fill the jars with water." They obeyed, filling them right to the brim. "Draw out now," commanded Jesus, "and bring it to the chief steward."

The water was water no longer. It had become very good wine! The chief steward did not know where the wine had come from. He tasted it and marveled at the excellence of its taste. He called the bridegroom and said, "Every man at first sets forth the good wine and when they have drunk freely, the poorer wine. But you have kept the good wine until now."

This was Jesus' first miracle. He showed his glory, and his disciples believed in him. Through Mary's intercession, Jesus worked his first miracle.

Only God can work miracles. With this miracle, Jesus showed the world that he is God.

The Lord is my shepherd; I shall not want.
He guides me in right paths for his name's sake.
Even though I walk in the dark valley
I fear no evil; for you are at my side.
Only goodness and kindness follow me
all the days of my life;
And I shall dwell in the house of the Lord
for years to come.

Psalm 22

Jesus' Miracles

The Miraculous Catch of Fish

The scene of the miraculous catch of fish was Lake Genesareth, which is also called the Sea of Galilee. While the crowds were pressing upon Jesus to hear the word of God, he was standing by the lake. What a touching sight the sincere Galileans must have made as they crowded about Jesus to hear his words of eternal life! Their eagerness to hear him caused the Master to make a decision. He saw two boats moored by the lake, but the fishermen had left them and were washing their nets. And getting into one of the boats, the one that was Simon's he asked him to put out a little from the land. And sitting down, he began to teach the crowds from the boat. Why did Jesus choose Peter's boat? To tell everyone that his word is preached only from the boat of Peter. Peter's boat is the Church.

When Jesus had stopped speaking, he said to Simon, "Put out into the deep and lower your nets for a catch." And Simon answered and said to him, "Master, the whole night through we have worked hard and have taken nothing; but at your word I will lower the net." And when they had done so, they enclosed such a great number of fish that their net began to break. And they waved to their friends in the other boat to come and help them. And they came and filled both the boats, so that they began to sink.

Seeing the miraculous catch, Simon Peter fell down at Jesus' knees, saying, "Depart from me, for I am a sinful man, O Lord." And Jesus said to Simon, "Do not be afraid; from now on, you will catch men." And when they had brought their boats to land, they left all and followed him.

This was how Jesus called Peter and the other apostles. Jesus addresses the same call to the apostles of our times; perhaps he is calling one of you?...

The Cure of a Deaf and Dumb Man

Jesus and his disciples had gone into the Phoenician territory of Tyre and Sidon on the Mediterranean, where he had cured the daughter of a Chanaanite woman. On the return journey, they walked through the mountainous region of the Decapolis, or Ten Cities, inhabited mainly by pagans. The news that he was passing by spread very swiftly. Everyone had now heard of Jesus' goodness, and they took the opportunity to bring to him the sick and the crippled. Among others, they brought to him one deaf and dumb, and asked him to lay his hand upon him. And taking him aside from the crowd, Jesus put his fingers into the man's ears and spitting, he touched his tongue. And looking up to heaven, he sighed, and said to him, "Be opened." And his ears were at once opened, and the bond of his tongue loosed, and he began to speak correctly.

Deafness is a great misfortune; it is even more so when there is lack of speech, because in this manner two great means of communication and expression are lacking to the poor person. Spiritual deafness and dumbness are very serious, too. The *spiritually deaf* are those who no longer hear either the voice of conscience or the voice of God calling them through the wonders of nature, the beauties of religion and the examples of the saints.

But Jesus is always ready to perform miracles. He invites such souls to step aside, because in the midst of the confusion of the world, his voice cannot be heard; then he cures them through the great power of his sacraments. In the miracle of the deaf mute, Jesus made use of outward signs. He touched the

108

man's ears with his fingers, he moistened his tongue with his saliva and said, "Be opened!" to work this miracle of his almighty power. How beautifully his actions symbolize the sacraments. The sacraments are signs which tell us that they are producing grace in the soul.

The Blind Man at Jericho

One day the Savior came to Jericho. A blind man was begging along the roadside. Hearing the crowd pass, he asked what was going on, and they told him that Jesus of Nazareth was passing by. At this news, his heart was filled with hope. He was tired of living in the dark, full of misery and discomfort. He wanted to see the light. Therefore, he began to cry out: "Jesus, Son of David, have mercy on me!" Instead of encouraging him, the crowd that followed Jesus scolded him to silence him. But his faith overcame every obstacle and he shouted louder still: "Son of David, have mercy on me!"

Jesus heard his cry. He stopped and commanded that the blind man be brought to him. "What would you have me do for you?" Jesus asked.

And the man said, "Lord, that I may see."

Jesus rewarded his faith: "Receive your sight, your faith has saved you." Immediately the blind man's sight was restored, and he followed Jesus, full of gratitude and joy. Upon seeing the miracle, all the people gave praise to God.

The blind man is a symbol of the sinner whose soul is in darkness. The soul is created for God. Only God can satisfy it. What should a person do when he finds himself in a state of sin? He must overcome all obstacles, turn to Jesus and say: "Lord, that I may see!"

One night, after a very full day of teaching beside Lake Genesareth, the Divine Master and his disciples set out to cross the lake. Jesus lay down in the stern, or back, of the boat and fell fast asleep. He was tired!

Suddenly a great wind arose. The wild gusts followed one another rapidly. Beaten and dragged about, the small boat began to ship water on all sides. Although the disciples were seasoned sailors and used to these sudden Galilean storms, they now became very much afraid. Jesus continued to sleep. The disciples worked feverishly with their arms and their oars, battling fiercely against the waves, but when suddenly the boat seemed about to be sunk, they could hold themselves back no longer; shaking Jesus, they shouted: "Lord, save us! We are perishing!"

Without becoming excited, Jesus answered them: "Why are you fearful, O you of little faith?" Then He arose and rebuked the wind and the sea; and instantly there came a great calm; the wind ceased and the waves became still. At this new sign of divine power, the disciples were filled with wonder and said to themselves: "What manner of Man is this, that even the wind and the sea obey him?"

That storm-battered boat symbolizes the Church, which crosses the sea of the present life amidst alternating periods of calm and stormy weather. How many times the faithful have had to raise their cries for help to Jesus, apparently asleep in the Church, during dangers, persecutions and battles which seemed to submerge all of Christianity! When all seemed lost, Jesus spoke one word and calm was restored. The boat of Peter has continued to sail gloriously through the centuries; it will continue its course until the end of time, because the apostles are rowing it while Jesus rests in it.

The Multiplication of the Loaves

The people loved Jesus greatly and followed him without becoming tired. From every part of Palestine, they hurried to him to hear his words of eternal life. One time, Jesus left the shore and went up a mountain with his disciples. The crowds followed him. When Jesus saw all those people, he smiled kindly and spoke of the Kingdom of Heaven. Now when it was evening, the disciples went to the Master, and suggested that it might be well to dismiss the crowds, so that they might go to nearby villages to buy food. That spot was a desert place.

But Jesus said to Philip, "You yourselves give food to these people. How much bread do you have?"

"Master," replied the apostle, "two hundred denarii worth of bread is not enough for them, that each may receive a little."

Andrew, the brother of Simon, said, "There is a young boy here who has five barley loaves and two fishes. But what are these among so many people?"

"Make the people sit down on the grass," Jesus told them.

The people sat down in groups. There were five thousand, not counting the women and children. When they were seated, Jesus took the five loaves, looked toward heaven and gave thanks. Then he broke the bread and had it distributed to the people to take as much as they wished.

When everyone was filled, Jesus said to his disciples, "Gather the fragments that are left over, lest they be wasted." The disciples obeyed and they gathered no less than twelve baskets of leftovers! Having seen this miracle, the people cried out happily, "This is indeed the prophet who was to come into the world—the Messia!" And they wanted to take him by force and make him king. However, Jesus wanted to be king of our hearts, not an earthly king. Therefore, he told his disciples to send the people home and to cross over to the other shore of the lake. Jesus meanwhile fled up the mountain alone.

The crowds were waiting at the lake shore for Jesus to come down the mountain. But they waited in vain. Astonished, they crossed over the next day to the opposite shore, looking for Jesus. They found him in the synagogue of Capharnaum. "Master," they asked, "when did You come here?"

"Truly, truly, I say to you," replied Jesus, "you look for me because you have eaten of the loaves and have been filled. Do not labor for the food that perishes but for that which lasts for life everlasting, which the Son of Man will give you."

"Lord," they begged, "give us always this bread."

Then Jesus said, "I am the bread of life. He who comes to me shall not hunger, and he who believes in me shall never thirst. If anyone eat of this bread, he shall live forever; and the bread that I will give is my flesh for the life of the world."

The Jews began to argue with one another, saying, "How can this man give us his flesh to eat?"

But Jesus told them, "Truly, truly, I say to you, unless you eat the flesh of the Son of Man, and drink his blood, you shall not have life in you. He who eats my flesh and drinks my blood has life everlasting and I will raise him up on the last day".

Do you know what bread Jesus was talking about?...He was talking about the Holy Eucharist, which he was to institute at the Last Supper!

The Widow's Son

One day Jesus went to a town called Naim, and his disciples and a large crowd went with him. As he drew near the gate of the town, he saw a dead man being carried out, the only son of his mother, and she was a widow. A large gathering from the town was with her.

A funeral is always sad, especially when it is the funeral of a young son....The dead man of Naim was still young. He was rich, too, and the only son of his mother, who loved him dearly and had not spared any expense to cure him. And yet he had died. Do we ever think about death? The prophet Isaia said, "The life of man is like a flower, which lives for a short time, then withers and dies".

Seeing that poor mother, the Lord had compassion on her, and said to her, "Do not weep." And he went up and touched the stretcher, and the bearers stood still. "Young man," he said, "I say to you, arise." And he who was dead, sat up and began to speak. Then Jesus gave him to his mother.

The tears of that mother had deeply touched the heart of Jesus. When he looked at the woman, his gaze was like a ray of sunlight. He told her not to weep—words which only he could say, because no one but he could give back to her that son over whom she was weeping.

When we are in deep sorrow, to whom should we go for consolation?... We should go to Jesus, for he is God. He alone can dry our tears.

The Raising of Lazarus

Lazarus and his sisters, Martha and Mary, were followers of Jesus. They lived in Bethany, a village very near Jerusalem. Jesus loved Lazarus and his two sisters dearly; he often went to their home to speak to them of the Kingdom of God and to rest a while with his disciples.

Once when Jesus was far away from Bethany, Lazarus became seriously sick. Martha and Mary sent an urgent message: "Lord, he whom you love is sick."

"This sickness," replied Jesus, "is not unto death but for the glory of God, that through it, the Son of God may be glorified."

By the time the message reached Jesus, Lazarus was already dead; Jesus knew that. But even though Jesus loved Lazarus very much, he waited two more days before setting out for Bethany. Then he said to his disciples, "Let us go again into Judea."

"Master," objected his disciples, "just now the Jews were seeking to stone you and do you go there again?

"Our friend Lazarus is dead," Jesus told them. "But let us go to him."

When Jesus reached Bethany, he found that Lazarus had already been in his grave four days. Many people had gathered in the home of Martha and Mary to console the sisters. As soon as Martha heard that Jesus was coming, she went out to meet him and said, "Lord, if you had been here, my brother would not have died. But even now, I know that whatever you ask of God, God will give it to you."

"Your brother shall rise," was Jesus' answer. Then, deeply touched, he asked, "Where have you laid him?"

"Lord, come and see."

And Jesus wept. "See how much he loved Lazarus," people whispered.

Jesus went to the tomb, which was a cave with a stone laid against the opening.

"Take away the stone," the Lord commanded.

"Lord, by this time he is already decayed, for he is dead four days," pointed out Martha.

"Have I not told you that, if you believe, you shall see the glory of God?" Jesus answered.

So they removed the stone. Then he cried out with a loud voice, "Lazarus, come forth!"

At once the man who had been dead came out of his tomb, his hands and feet bound with strips of cloth and his face covered.

"Unbind him and let him go," commanded Jesus.

Having witnessed such a shocking miracle, many of the people who had followed Jesus to the sepulchre believed in him.

These were only a few of the many miracles that Jesus worked. St. John said that if everything Jesus did had been written down, the whole world would not be able to hold all the books.

You are my God, and I give thanks to you;
O my God, I praise you.

Psalm 117

What Jesus Taught

The Sermon on the Mount

Often Jesus would go apart from his disciples to spend the whole night praying. On the morning after one such night, he chose twelve of his disciples to follow him in a special way. Meanwhile, a great crowd came toward him from the nearby villages.

When Jesus saw the crowd, he went up a mountain. After he had sat down, his disciples gathered around, with the people behind them. Then he began to teach them:

"Blessed are the poor in spirit, for theirs is the kingdom of heaven.

Blessed are the meek, for they shall possess the earth.

Blessed are they who mourn, for they shall be comforted.

Blessed are they who hunger and thirst for justice, for they shall be satisfied.

Blessed are the merciful, for they shall obtain mercy.

Blessed are the clean of heart, for they shall see God.

Blessed are the peacemakers, for they shall be called children of God.

Blessed are they who suffer persecution for justice' sake, for theirs is the kingdom of heaven.

Blessed are you when men reproach you, and persecute you, and, speaking falsely, say all manner of evil against you, for my sake. Rejoice and exult, because your reward is great in heaven"

117

What peace and joy those poor, tired peasant people must have felt to hear those words — to hear that all their good deeds and all the sorrows they had to bear would someday win them happiness! And Jesus spoke on, in the sermon which contains such wonderful teachings about a good Christian life. He told his disciples that they — and we — should let everyone see the goodness of our lives, just as a city built on a hilltop can be seen for miles around.

Then Jesus warned against THE DANGER OF DOING GOOD THINGS—such as helping others or praying—FOR THE WRONG PURPOSE. These things should be done to please God. If, instead, we do them so that others will say how good we are, God our Father will not reward us.

He spoke about the Old Law given by God through Moses on another mountain, Mount Sinai, and said that he had come to make that Law completely perfect. Those who keep all the Commandments will be the greatest in the Kingdom of Heaven.

AND THEN JESUS SPOKE ABOUT ANGER: "You have heard the commandment given to our forefathers, 'You shall not kill.' Every murderer will be judged. But now I warn you, everyone who becomes angry with his brother will be judged. Therefore, if at the moment you are bringing your gifts to the altar, you recall that your brother has anything against you, leave your gift before the altar and go first to be reconciled to your brother. Then come and offer your gift."

Jesus next warned us TO BE PURE IN THOUGHT AND BODY, and to avoid everything which could lead us into impurity.

He told us TO TURN THE OTHER CHEEK if someone hits us on one—that is, to take insults or other injuries calmly and even to be ready for more. He told us always to be ready to do a favor when asked, and to give even more help than we have to give.

And then Jesus went even further. He told us TO LOVE OUR ENEMIES, to do good to those who hate us and to pray for those who call us names or make fun of us or hurt us in other ways. He said that it is not enough to love those who love us. We must love everyone in the world, because God the Father loves everyone, and we must become as much like God the Father as we can.

At this point Jesus taught THE BEST OF ALL PRAYERS, THE OUR FATHER:

Our Father, who art in heaven,
hallowed be thy name;
> (hallowed means honored or praised)

thy kingdom come;
> (this kingdom means God's reign in the hearts of all men, so that he will be worshiped by all)

thy will be done on earth as it is in heaven.
> (will means plan or purpose)

Give us this day our daily bread;
> (this daily bread includes the food, clothing and shelter we need, and especially the graces our souls need)

And forgive us our trespasses as we forgive those who trespass against us;
> (trespasses are injuries of any sort)

And lead us not into temptation,
> (temptation is an encouragement to commit sin)

But deliver us from evil. Amen.
> (deliver means to free; amen means let it be this way)

Jesus himself explained the last words of the Our Father to us, saying that if we do not forgive others, our Father in heaven will not forgive us.

The next thing Jesus said in this great Sermon on the Mount REMINDS US OF HIS REASON FOR BEING BORN POOR. He said that the good things of this world do not last and that the only real treasure is heaven. Our hearts should desire heaven, and we should serve only God, so as to win eternal happiness.

And then Jesus said something very beautiful about HAVING TRUST IN GOD: "Do not be anxious for your life, what you shall eat; nor yet for your body, what you shall put on. Is not the life a greater thing than the food, and the body than the clothing? Look at the birds of the air: they do not sow, or reap, or gather into barns; yet your heavenly Father feeds them. Are not you of much more value than they? But which of you by being anxious about it can add anything to his height?

"And as for clothing, why are you anxious? Consider how the lilies of the field grow. They do not toil; they do not spin thread. Yet I say to you that not even Solomon in all his glory was arrayed like one of these. But if God so clothes the grass of the field, which flourishes today but tomorrow is thrown into the oven, how much more you, O you of little faith!

"Therefore do not be anxious, saying, 'What shall we eat?' or, 'What shall we drink?' or, 'What are we to put on?' (for after all these things the pagans seek); for your Father knows that you need all these things. But seek first the Kingdom of God and his justice, and all these things shall be given you besides."

FIRST COMES SALVATION OF THE SOUL; everything else is much less important. We must first of all seek heaven and perform good works to attain it, and then think of the other things. God has given us the use of reason to plan for the future but it is a sign of wisdom to provide first for the soul, then for the body.

In that beautiful Sermon on the Mount Jesus also taught that we all have so many faults that WE SHOULD NEVER TALK ABOUT THE FAULTS OF OTHERS, and that WE SHOULD DO TO EACH PERSON WHAT WE WOULD WISH THAT PERSON TO DO TO US. We call this the golden rule: "Do to others as you would have them do to you."

We MUST PRAY ALWAYS, Jesus taught. If we ask, we will receive; if we seek, or look for, we will find; if we knock, the door will be opened to us.

If we listen to Jesus' words and do what he has told us, we will be happy. Jesus declared that someone who hears his words and acts upon them is like a wise man who built his house on a rock. When storms and floods came, the house was safe. Someone who does not obey Jesus' words is like a foolish man who built his house on a hill of sand. The storms and floods swept the sand hill away, and the house collapsed and was ruined.

That was how Jesus ended the Sermon on the Mount. He has shown us God's love for us poor sinners and has taught us to return this love of God and to imitate God our Father's love by loving everyone in the world. The people who had listened to the sermon were filled with amazement because Jesus spoke as a person who had authority. Jesus did not speak like other prophets, saying, "The Lord says this." Instead, Jesus said, *"I* say to you." He taught in his own name because he is God.

Jesus and the Children

Jesus traveled tirelessly all over Palestine, preaching the Kingdom of Heaven. The apostles followed him enthusiastically, treasuring every word he said.

On one occasion, however, the apostles let Jesus walk ahead alone, while they followed at a distance, arguing excitedly. They did not want Jesus to hear their discussion. But Jesus is God and he read their minds and hearts.

When they reached home, he asked them: What were you talking about on the way?

The apostles looked at each other, embarrassed. Finally they said: "Master, who will be the greatest in the Kingdom of Heaven?"

That was the topic of their argument: who was to be the greatest! So Jesus called a child, set him in their midst, in the place of honor, and pointing to him, said, "Amen I say to you, unless you change and become like little children, you will not enter into the Kingdom of Heaven."

Jesus was talking to grown men. How were they to change and become small again, like that little child? Jesus was not speaking of the size of children. He was speaking of child-like innocence and simplicity.

Then he said sternly, "Woe to whoever causes one of these little ones who believe in me to sin!"

"See that you do not despise one of these little ones," Jesus said, "for I tell you, their angels in heaven always behold the face of my Father in heaven".

See how much Jesus thinks of children; and how much he loves them! They are his joy, all his delight.

The children knew they were Jesus' special friends, his favorites, and when they would hear that the Master was coming, they would run to meet him joyfully.

On one occasion, Jesus had preached and worked many miracles and was tired. He stopped to rest a while. The chil-

dren took their chance to crowd all around him, to look right up into his eyes, and receive his pats and his blessings.

The apostles thought those children must surely have been annoying the Master, so they tried to send them away.

"Go away, you pests! The Master is tired! Go home!"

But Jesus warned the apostles. "No! No!" he said. "Let the little children come to me, and do not prevent them, for of such is the Kingdom of God."

The children who are closest to Jesus, who receive him in Holy Communion and who talk and listen to him, receive from him the most graces and blessings.

Jesus Proclaims the Foundation of His Church

When Jesus and his disciples were in the district of Caesarea Philippi, he began to ask them, "Who do men say the Son of Man is?"

They answered, "Some say, John the Baptist; others, Elia; and others Jeremia or another of the prophets."

"But who do you say that I am?" Jesus asked.

Simon Peter answered and said, "You are the Christ, the Son of the living God."

Then Jesus said, "Blessed are you, Simon son of John, for flesh and blood have not revealed this to you, but my Father in heaven. And I say to you, you are Peter, and upon this rock I will build my Church, and the gates of hell shall not prevail against it. And I will give you the keys of the Kingdom of Heaven; and whatever you will bind on earth will be bound in heaven, and whatever you will loose on earth will be loosed in heaven."

After Peter's solemn confession of the divinity of Christ, Jesus promised to establish his Church, that is, the community of his followers.

At the head of his Church, Jesus Christ placed Peter and the apostles. The successor of Peter is the Pope. Like Peter, the Pope is the Vicar of Jesus Christ. The Pope acts in the place of Christ; he represents him.

Jesus guides us by means of his Church.

The successors of the apostles are the bishops. Just as one who rebels against his own general is not a good soldier, so

124

one who does not obey the Pope and the bishops is not a good Christian.

The Heavenly Father Shows That Jesus Is God

One day Jesus wanted to give his apostles a peek at his glory. He took Peter, James and John, and went up a mountain to pray. It was night. Jesus prayed. The apostles sleepily waited for him at a little distance.

Towards dawn, a blinding light awakened them. During his prayers, Jesus had become transfigured. His face shone as the sun and his garments became white as snow. Throughout his mortal life, Jesus had constantly hidden his divinity. Now, however, he let it be seen for a moment.

Two men were talking with him. These were Moses and Elia, who, appearing in glory, spoke of Jesus' death.

Overjoyed by the heavenly vision, Peter exclaimed: "Lord, it is good for us to be here. If you wish, let us set up three tents here, one for you, one for Moses, and one for Elia."

And as Peter was still speaking, a bright cloud over-shadowed them, and a voice out the cloud said, "This is my beloved Son, in whom I am well pleased; hear him!" For the second time the heavenly Father acknowledged his beloved Son and presented him to the world. Our heavenly Father showed us that Jesus is our Master. He is the Way, the Truth and the Life. He is the Truth that "enlightens every man that comes into this world." He is the only Way that leads to the Father. He is the Life of the soul: "He who follows me does not walk in the darkness, but will have the light of life."

The purpose of the Transfiguration of Jesus was to remove the fear of the cross from the minds of the disciples. It was to give them a strong hope of enjoying the happiness of heaven after they had followed Jesus in his sufferings.

Jesus Christ Speaks about His Father

"Let not your heart be troubled," Jesus once told the apostles. "You believe in God, believe also in me. In my Father's house there are many rooms. If there were not, I would have told you, because I go to prepare a place for you. And if I go and prepare a place for you, I am coming again, and I will take you to myself; that where I am, there you also may be. And where I go you know, and the way you know."

Thomas said to him, "Lord, we do not know where you are going, and how can we know the way?" Jesus said to him, "I am the Way, and the Truth, and the Life. No one comes to the Father except through me. If you had known me, you would also have known my Father. And from now on, you will know him. You have seen him."

Philip said to him, "Lord, show us the Father and it is enough for us." Jesus said to him, "Have I been so long a time with you, and you have not known me? Philip, he who sees me sees me sees also the Father. How can you say, 'Show us the Father?' Do you not believe that I am in the Father and the Father in me? The words that I speak to you I speak not on my own authority. But the Father living in me does the works. Do you believe that I am in the Father and the Father in me?

"If anyone loves me, he will keep my word, and my Father will love him, and we will come to him and make our home with him. He who does not love me does not keep my words. And the word that you have heard is not mine, but the Father's who sent me.

"These things I have spoken to you while yet with you. But the Advocate, the Holy Spirit, whom the Father will send in my name, will teach you all things, and bring to your mind whatever I have said to you.

"Peace I leave with you, my peace I give to you; not as the world gives do I give to you. Do not let your heart be troubled or afraid."

With this beautiful talk Jesus comforts us, too, for he tells us that after this short life he will give us, too, a beautiful place he has prepared for us in heaven.

Jesus Master, you are the Christ, the Son of the living God.
Only you have words of eternal life.
Matthew 16; John 6

The Parables of Jesus

The Great Supper

Jesus had been invited to a supper and during the course of the banquet he gave lessons on humility: "When you are invited, do not sit in the first place, but in the last place..." and on generous charity: "Do not invite your friends, but the poor who cannot repay you."

One of the guests, excited by the teachings of Jesus, exclaimed: "Blessed is he who shall feast in the Kingdom of God!" Jesus answered him by telling a parable, or story with a special meaning. The story told an important truth.

"A certain man," he said, "gave a great supper, and he invited many. And he sent his servant at supper time to tell those invited to come, for everything was now ready."

The man who gives the supper is Jesus; the banquet to which he invited all men is the Kingdom of God and the Eucharistic Banquet. Everyone is invited.

"And," Jesus went on, "they all with one accord began to excuse themselves. The first said, 'I have bought a farm, and I must go out and see it; I beg you to excuse me.' And another said, 'I have bought five yokes of oxen, and I am on my way to try them; I beg you to excuse me.' And another said, 'I have married a wife, and therefore I cannot come.'"

When the servant told the master of the house about these excuses, the master ordered him to go and call other people: "Go out quickly into the streets and lanes of the city, and bring in here the poor, and the crippled, and the blind, and the lame." And as there was still room, the master sent the servant out a third time to call others: "Go out into the highways and hedges, and make them come in, so that my house may be filled."

Who are represented by these poor people who filled the house of the master? They are the humble, the suffering, the simple people. These are the privileged souls who have the honor of sitting at the Eucharistic Banquet and who receive the promise of future glory!

The Good Samaritan

A doctor of the law tested Jesus with this question: "Master, what must I do to gain eternal life?"

Jesus answered him by asking a question: "What is written in the Law? What do your read there?" Well instructed on this point, the lawyer answered: "You shall love the Lord your God with your whole heart, and with your whole soul, and with your strength, and with your whole mind; and your neighbor as yourself."

Jesus replied, "You have answered rightly; do this and you shall live."

But he said to Jesus, "And who is my neighbor?"

Jesus answered with one of the most beautiful parables: "A certain man was going down from Jerusalem to Jericho, and he fell in with robbers, who after stripping him and beating him went their way, leaving him half-dead. But, as it happened, a certain priest was going down the same way, and when he saw him, he passed by. And likewise a Levite also, when he was near the place and saw him, passed by. But a certain Samaritan as he journeyed came upon him, and seeing him, was moved with compassion. And he went up to him and bound up his wounds, pouring on oil and wine. And setting him on his own beast, he brought him to an inn and took care of him. And the next day he took out two denarii and gave them to the innkeeper and said, 'Take care of him; and whatever more you spend, I, on my way back will repay you.'

"Which of these three," Jesus asked the lawyer, "in your opinion, proved himself neighbor to him who fell among the robbers?"

And the lawyer answered, "He who took pity on him." And Jesus said to him, "Go and do the same yourself."

With this parable Jesus teaches us that everyone, regardless of race and color, and even an enemy, is our neighbor. And he tells us to love everyone. Christian love is not based on the good or bad qualities of our neighbor; it takes root in God, who is the Father of all mankind and who considers whatever we do to our brothers as done to himself.

Jesus used to welcome sinners as a doctor welcomes the sick. "The Son of Man came to save what was lost," he said. Comforted by the word of eternal life, the sinners opened their hearts to Jesus.

The scribes and pharisees, who would never have gone near a sinner, were horrified by the conduct of Jesus. He answered their murmurings with a parable which shows God's mercy. A parable is a comparison in which a great truth is hidden.

"What man of you having a hundred sheep, and losing one of them, does not leave the ninety-nine in the desert, and go after that which is lost, until he finds it? And when he has found it, he lays it upon his shoulders rejoicing. And on coming home he calls together his friends and neighbors, saying to them, 'Rejoice with me, because I have found my sheep that was lost.' I say to you that, even so, there will be joy in heaven over one sinner who repents, more than over ninety-nine good people who have no need of repentance."

The meaning of this parable is very simple. Jesus is the Shepherd. The lost sheep is the sinner. The Savior feels sorry for the soul which has fallen into sin. He follows it and calls it; he gives himself no peace until he has succeeded in saving it. Upon finding it, he does not beat it or scold it; he lifts it up and carries it on his shoulders, inviting all heaven to rejoice with him. Could the Divine Master have drawn a more tender picture of the loving care which he has for the sinner?

The Pharisee and the Publican

The parable of the Pharisee and of the Publican presents to us two men who pray to God in completely different ways. The Pharisee represents the hypocrite, or faker, who tries only to make a good impression. He is a model of the proud man who despises others. The Publican, instead, is the model of the repentant sinner; he is a man who examines his own conscience, and humbly asks for the mercy of the Lord.

Jesus said, "Two men went up to the Temple to pray, the one a Pharisee and the other a Publican. The Pharisee stood and began to pray thus within himself: 'O God, I thank you that I am not like the rest of men, robbers, dishonest, adulterers, or even like this Publican. I fast twice a week; I pay tithes of all that I possess.'"

But what kind of prayer is this? Above all, notice the position taken by this proud Pharisee. He enters the Temple with head held high, casts a scornful glance at the Publican and keeps his head up in the presence of the supreme majesty of God. And what does he say? He thanks God because he is better than others. He does not ask for graces; he acts as if he does not need graces. He praises himself and compares himself with others, finding them all unjust; he alone is holy.

The Publican acts in a completely different way: "Standing afar off, he would not so much as lift up his eyes to heaven, but kept striking his breast, saying, 'O God, be merciful to me the sinner!'"

Here is a picture of a penitent sinner. He is a sinner; he knows it and is ashamed of it. He feels unworthy of being in a holy place and does not even dare to raise his eyes up to heaven. He looks into the depths of his soul, sees his sins, beats his breast as though to punish himself, and finds refuge in the mercy of God.

Jesus, the just Judge, concluded the parable with this sentence: "I tell you, this man (the Publican) went back to his home forgiven. The Pharisee, instead, went back home a greater sinner than before; for everyone who is proud of himself shall be humbled, and he who humbles himself shall be raised up."

Parable of the Sower

One day Jesus told this parable to a great crowd who surrounded him: "The farmer went out to sow his seed. And as he sowed, some seed fell by the wayside and was stamped under foot, and the birds of the air ate it up. And other seed fell upon the rock, and as soon as it had sprung up it withered away, because it had no moisture. And other seed fell among thorns, and the thorns sprang up with it and choked it. And other seed fell upon good ground, and sprang up and yielded good fruit a hundredfold."

After the crowd had left, the disciples asked Jesus the meaning of this parable. Then Jesus explained, "The seed is the word of God. And those by the wayside are they who have heard. Then the devil comes and takes away the word from their heart, that they may not believe and be saved. Now those upon the

rock are they who, when they have heard, receive the word with joy; and these have no root, but believe for a while, and in time of temptation fall away. And that which fell among the thorns, these are they who have heard, and as they go their way are choked by the cares and riches and pleasures of life, and their fruit does not ripen. But that upon good ground, these are they who, with a right and good heart, having heard the word, hold it fast, and bear fruit in patience".

The word of God is the great gift which Jesus came upon the earth to bring. But this wonderful gift can be lost, just as a seed may simply lie in the ground after the farmer has planted it. In order that the divine seed may grow and produce fruit, we must welcome it when we learn about it in religion class, hear it in sermons or read it in books. We must think about God's word and pray to remember it. And we must be brave enough to do what Jesus wants all the time.

Parables of the Kingdom

Jesus said: "The Kingdom of Heaven is like a man who sowed good seed in his field. But while men were asleep his enemy came and sowed weeds among the wheat, and went away. And when the blades sprang up and brought forth fruit, then the weeds appeared as well. And the servants of the landowner came and said to him: 'Sir, did you not sow good seed in your field? How then does it have weeds? Will you have us go and gather them up?'

"'No,' he said, 'lest in gathering the weeds you root up the wheat along with them. Let both grow together until the harvest. And at harvest time I will say to the reapers: 'Gather up first the weeds, and bind them in bundles to burn; but the wheat gather into my barn'."

This parable explains why there is so much evil in this world, even among Catholics. It is the work of the devil. But God does not punish the wicked immediately. He gives them time to realize their mistakes and to do penance: "I do not want the death of a sinner," he said, "but that he be converted and be

134

saved" (see Ezechiel 33:11). How many sinners, who were like weeds in the field of God, changed their ways and became great saints! Among them were King David, St. Augustine, Mary Magdalene and the good thief, for example.

Jesus spoke another parable:

"The Kingdom of Heaven," he said, "is like a grain of mustard seed, which a man took and sowed in his field. This indeed is the smallest of all the seeds; but when it grows up it is larger than any herb and becomes a tree, so that the birds of the air come and live in its branches." The grain of mustard seed is a symbol of the *Church* that Jesus founded.

In the beginning the Church was like a grain of mustard seed. Jesus had told the apostles: "They have persecuted me, they will also persecute you." How many persecutions the Church has endured down through the centuries! But the Church always wins; she continues to extend her great branches over all the world, and *the birds of the air,* that is, the souls, find peace and security in her.

Jesus also spoke another parable: "The Kingdom of God is like yeast, which a woman took and buried in three measures of flour, until all of it was leavened." The activity of the yeast represents the Church's activity in transforming the world by the preaching of the Holy Gospel.

We believe in our Lord Jesus Christ,
who is the Son of God.
He lived among us, full of grace and truth.
He proclaimed and established the Kingdom of God,
and made us know in himself the Father.
He gave us his new commandment —
to love one another as he loved us.

Credo of the People of God

The End of the World

One day Jesus spoke to his disciples about the end of the world. He said: "The sun will be darkened, and the moon will not give her light, and the stars will fall from heaven, and the powers of heaven will be shaken. And then will appear the sign of the Son of Man in heaven; and then will all tribes of the earth mourn, and they will see the Son of Man coming upon the clouds of heaven with great power and majesty! And he will send forth his angels with a trumpet and a great sound, and they will gather his chosen ones from the four winds, from one end of the heavens to the other."

"The Son of Man will sit on the throne of his glory; and before him will be gathered all the nations, and he will separate them one from another, as the shepherd separates the sheep from the goats; and he will set the sheep on his right hand, but the goats on the left. Then the King will say to those on his right hand, 'Come blessed of my Father, take possession of the kingdom prepared for you from the foundation of the world.... Then he will say to those on his left hand, 'Depart from me, accursed ones, into the everlasting fire which was prepared for the devil and his angels.... And these will go into everlasting punishment, but the just into everlasting life.'

"Heaven and earth will pass away, but my words will not pass away."

The account of the end of the world and the Universal Judgment should not frighten us. Jesus gave us this warning so that we would be on guard, always ready, as though the end of the world were about to come for each one of us from one moment to the other. Does it not come, in fact, with death?

Our Redemption

Jesus Enters Jerusalem in Triumph

One sad day, Jesus said to his apostles, "Behold, we are going up to Jerusalem, and all things that have been written by the prophets concerning the Son of Man will be accomplished. He will be betrayed to the chief priests and the scribes, and they will condemn him to death and will deliver him to the pagans to be mocked and scourged and crucified. But on the third day he will rise again." When they were near Jerusalem two disciples brought to him the colt of a donkey. They spread their cloaks on it, and Jesus mounted. As he rode ahead, so humble a King, the crowds spread their cloaks in his path and cut palm branches to wave. "Hosanna!" they cried joyfully. "Blessed is the King who comes in the name of the Lord! Hosanna in the highest!"

When the people, and particularly the children, heard that Jesus was arriving in Jerusalem, they hurried to meet him with palm branches and flowers. Joyously they shouted, "Hosanna to the Son of David! Blessed is he who comes in the name of the Lord! Hosanna! Hosanna!"

Thus, a long procession formed and the people in front and behind glorified the King of Israel. In triumph Jesus came to Jerusalem. Yet on seeing the city, Jesus felt sad and he wept. He went on into the city, blessing everyone as he passed by. Great was the gratitude of the crowd, who were praising the infinite goodness of the Savior. Their joy was intense.

"Rejoice greatly, O daughter of Sion! Shout for joy, O daughter of Jerusalem!" the prophet had said. "Behold your King will come to you, the Just and Savior! He is poor, and riding upon a donkey, and upon a colt, the foal of a donkey.... He shall speak peace to the pagans, and his power shall be from sea to sea, even to the end of the earth".

Great conquerors ride on proud steeds and are surrounded by the homage of the conquered. Jesus rode on a humble donkey in order to tell everyone that his Kingdom is one of love and of peace. A few days later, our King, who had entered the Holy City in triumph, would be seen hanging crucified between two thieves. From that cross, which was his throne, he sealed his law of love.

Meanwhile, the chief priests and scribes were looking for a way to take Jesus prisoner. They were being careful, because they feared what the people might do. Their problem was solved when Satan entered into Judas Iscariot, who was greedy for money. Judas presented himself to the chief priests and said to them, "What are you willing to give me for delivering Jesus to you?" They offered thirty pieces of silver, and Judas sealed the bargain. From that moment on, he sought an opportunity to betray his Master.

Jesus' Last Supper with His Apostles

It was Thursday, the day on which the Jews sacrificed the passover lamb. Jesus wanted to make that supper a solemn one, for he knew what was going to take place and how memorable that supper would be. He called his two beloved disciples, Peter and John, and said to them, "Go and prepare for us the passover that we may eat it"

When evening came, our Savior reclined at table with his apostles and said to them, "I have greatly desired to eat this passover with you before I suffer; for I say to you that I will eat of it no more, until it has been fulfilled in the Kingdom of God"

The passover lamb had been eaten when, at a certain moment, Jesus rose from the table, wrapped himself with a towel, poured water into a basin, and began to wash the feet of the apostles.

Now after he had washed their feet, Jesus again reclined at table.

"Do you know what I have done to you?" he asked. "You call me Master and Lord, and you say well, for so I am. If, therefore, I the Lord and Master, have washed your feet, you also ought to wash the feet of one another. *For I have given you the example, that as I have done to you, so you also should do*"

After these lessons of humility and charity, Jesus grew serious and said sadly, "Amen, amen, I say to you, one of you will betray me!... The Son of Man indeed goes his way, as it is written of him, but woe to that man by whom the Christ is betrayed! It were better for that man if he had not been born."

Very much saddened, the apostles began to ask, "Is it I, Lord?" Even Juda had the boldness to ask him, and Jesus answered him softly, so that the others would not understand, "You have said it." Then after having given him, as a sign of love, bread which he had dipped for him, Jesus said to Judas, "What you do, do quickly."

After the traitor took that bite of bread, the devil took full possession of his soul, and Judas fled from the Cenacle to carry out the betrayal of Jesus. The departure of Judas brought relief to Jesus.

On that day when Jesus had multiplied the loaves of bread for the people, he had promised to give us heavenly bread to eat — the bread of eternal life. It was now the moment for him to fulfill his promise.

He took up unleavened bread (bread made without yeast), gave thanks, blessed it, broke it and gave it to his apostles, saying, *This is my Body,* which is being given for you." Then he took the chalice, gave thanks, blessed it, and gave it to them, saying, *This is my Blood* of the new covenant, which shall be shed for many, unto the forgiveness of sins." And he added, *"Do this in remembrance of me."*

"This is my Body, this is my Blood," Jesus had said. These simple, powerful words changed the substance of bread and wine into the Body and Blood of Jesus. The appearances of bread and wine, it is true, were not changed, yet the apostles believed what Jesus had said. How could they help but believe him? They knew he was God, infinitely powerful; they had seen him multiply bread more than once; they had seen him change water into wine, and most of all, they believed that Jesus loves us with an infinite love.

Jesus had told his apostles: *"Do this in remembrance of me."* The apostles and all their successors have obeyed the com-

mand of Jesus, repeating his words and renewing the great
mystery of the Last Supper. Every day, Jesus becomes present
with his Body, Blood, Soul and Divinity in every consecrated
Host.

When you look at the Sacred Host, your eyes see nothing
but a thin, round piece of bread. But those are only the appearances. The Holy Eucharist is not an image of Jesus as a crucifix
is; nor is it simply a memorial of his love for us. It is *really* Jesus,
the God-Man, whole and entire, living, glorious and immortal as
he is in heaven.

Our body needs food to keep alive and gain strength. The
soul, too, needs food to keep and increase sanctifying grace in
itself. And Jesus gave us this very food—the Holy Eucharist!

In the Holy Eucharist there is the same Jesus who was
born poor in the stable; whom the Blessed Virgin embraced and

141

presented to the shepherds; who lived in Nazareth as a simple laborer and preacher to the people of Palestine; who worked miracles for the poor, the sick and the afflicted; who tenderly loved children and sinners; who died on the cross for us — that very same Jesus, with his goodness, almighty power and love. He is not in a state of suffering, but *in a state of glory*, as he appeared to the apostles after his resurrection, and as he is in heaven.

Jesus Promises the Holy Spirit

That night Jesus told the apostles that the Holy Spirit would come soon. He encouraged them to be his witnesses. He comforted them and prepared them for the terrible persecutions of the future.

"If you love me," Jesus said, "keep my commandments. And I will ask the Father and he will give you another Advocate to dwell with you forever, the Spirit of truth whom the world cannot receive, because it neither sees him nor knows him. But you shall know him, because he will dwell with you, and be in you...."

"Peace I leave with you, my peace I give to you. Do not let your heart be troubled, or be afraid. You have heard me say to you, 'I go away and I am coming to you.' If you loved me, you would indeed rejoice that I am going to the Father. And now I have told you before it comes to pass, that when it has come to pass you may believe"

This was not the first time that Jesus had promised the coming of the Holy Spirit. With his light, the Holy Spirit would enlighten the minds of the apostles and of the faithful. Jesus called the Holy Spirit the *Spirit of Truth*, because he was to make known to the world the truths hidden in the mysteries of the Faith and would teach what is necessary for salvation. The Holy Spirit inspires holy thoughts in us, inflames our hearts with love, teaches us to pray, and gives us courage to do good.

Jesus Gives the Law of Love

"As the Father has loved me," Jesus said, "I also have loved you. Remain in my love. If you keep my commandments you will remain in my love, as I also have kept my Father's commandments and remain in his love. These things I have spoken to you that my joy may be in you, and that your joy may be made full.

"This is my commandment — that you love one another as I have loved you. Greater love than this no one has, that one lay down his life for his friends. You are my friends if you do the things I command you. No longer do I call you servants, because the servant does not know what his master does. But I have called you friends, because all things that I have heard from my Father I have made known to you. You have not chosen me, but I have chosen you, and have appointed you that you should go and bear fruit, and that your fruit should remain; that whatever you ask the Father in my name he may give you. These things I command you, that you may love one another" (John 15:9-17).

With these beautiful words Jesus taught us the way of salvation. To save our soul, we must keep God's Commandments. This way we also show that we really love God, who gave us his holy Commandments.

Jesus Consoles His Disciples

Knowing that he was soon to return to the Father, the Divine Master invited the apostles to look fearlessly into the future. Men had persecuted him; they would also persecute his followers. Because he could foresee this, Jesus warned his soldiers of the dangers and opposition that lay ahead of them:

"If the world hates you, know that it has hated me before you. If you were of the world, the world would love what is its own. But because you are not of the world, but I have chosen you out of the world, therefore the world hates you. Remember the word that I have spoken to you: No servant is greater than his master. If they have persecuted me, they will persecute you also; if they have kept my word, they will keep yours also. But all these things they will do to you for my name's sake, because they do not know him who sent me.

"They will send you out of the synagogues. Yes, the hour is coming for everyone who kills you to think that he is offering worship to God. And these things they will do because they have not known the Father nor me. But these things I have spoken to you, that when the time for them has come you may remember that I told you".

The history of the Church shows us how it has always been persecuted, as Jesus foretold.

From us, too, Jesus expects witness to the Faith. If we are chosen to suffer something for love of Jesus, let us not become discouraged; let us rejoice as the apostles did, remembering that Jesus, our glorious Leader, is with us to support us in the battle and to lead us to victory.

Jesus Announces His Return to the Father

The hour of the passion was drawing near. Having eaten his last supper with his apostles, Jesus was now walking with them to the Garden of Gethsemani. Along the way he prepared them for the terrible trial. In a hidden way, so as not to sadden them, he let them know what he was thinking about: "A little while and you shall see me no longer; and again a little while and you shall see me, because I go to the Father." Within a short while, he would be crucified and buried in a tomb, hidden from their sight. But then he would rise from the dead and they would see him again. With the words "I go to the Father," Jesus announced his ascension into heaven, which was to take place soon after his resurrection. In heaven his apostles would see him again and would reign with him forever.

The words spoken by Jesus to the apostles are also for us. The "little while" which separates us from the vision of God is our present life, which is always very short. Time goes by fast, and who can stop it? Now we see God through the curtain of faith; in a little while, in heaven, we shall see him face to face!

Jesus Prays in the Garden

Then Jesus went with his apostles to the Garden of Olives, called Gethsemani.

"Sit down here, while I go over there to pray," Jesus said to his disciples. Then, taking Peter, James and John, he went farther on into the garden. A great sadness came over his face. He was thinking of the serious sins of mankind, for which he would soon make reparation, and a strong feeling of dislike came over him.

"My soul is sad, even to death," he told the three apostles. "Wait here and watch with me." Going forward a little, Jesus prayed, "Father, if it is possible, let this cup pass away from me, yet not as I will, but as you will."

Falling into agony, Jesus prayed even harder. All over his body, his sweat became as drops of blood running down upon the ground. An angel came down from heaven to give him strength.

Then the Savior arose from prayer and went to his disciples. He found them sleeping.

145

"Rise, let us go," Jesus said to them. "He who betrays me is at hand."

Jesus suffered very, very much in the garden of Gethsemani, because he was not only truly God but also truly man like us. But he was ready to suffer and to die, because he wanted to obey his Father unto death. That was why he prayed: "Father, not as I will, but as you will." In the *Our Father* we, too, pray to be able always to do the holy will of God.

Jesus Lets Himself Be Taken

Jesus was still speaking when Judas arrived with a large crowd of people armed with swords and clubs and carrying lanterns. They had been sent by the chief priests and pharisees. Judas knew the garden well, for Jesus and his disciples had often met there to pray. The traitor had given this signal: "He whom I kiss is Jesus; take him and guard him carefully." Going right up to Jesus, then, the ungrateful traitor said, "Hail Rabbi!" and he kissed him.

"Judas," said Jesus, looking at him with pity, "do you betray the Son of Man with a kiss?" Then, turning to the crowd and the soldiers, he asked them, "Whom are you looking for?"

"Jesus of Nazareth!" was their reply.

"I am he," Jesus told them. As though struck by some powerful force, they all fell to the ground at his words.

"Whom do you seek?" the Savior asked again.

"Jesus of Nazareth!"

"I have told you that I am he," Jesus said. "If, therefore, you seek me, let these (the disciples) go their way." Peter drew his sword from its scabbard at that moment and struck the high priest's servant, named Malchus, cutting off his right ear. Jesus healed the servant with a miracle and then said to Peter, "Put up your sword into the scabbard. Do you suppose that I cannot ask my Father, and he will even now give me more than twelve legions of angels?"

Of his own free will, Jesus then let himself be taken, bound and dragged before one court after another. His disciples all left him and ran away.

On that sad night Jesus was first brought to Annas, an ex-high priest. Annas wanted to get Jesus to say something wrong, so he asked him many tricky questions about his teachings and his disciples.

"I have spoken openly to the world," replied Jesus. "Question those who have heard what I spoke to them. They know what I have said."

"Is that the way you answer the high priest?" one of Annas' servants shouted, jumping up. And with that, he slapped Jesus across the face so hard that it left a red mark.

Meekly Jesus said, "If I have spoken badly, point out the evil; but if well, why do you strike me?"

Seeing that he could come to no conclusion, Annas sent Jesus to the high priest Caiphas. With Caiphas was the Sanhedrin, that is, the religious court. All these men wanted to find a reason to put Jesus to death, but although many brought false witness against him, their evidence did not agree. Then Caiphas himself stood up and solemnly demanded, "I ask you solemnly by the living God to tell us whether you are the Christ, the Son of God."

"I am," Jesus answered. Instead of recognizing the truth of what Jesus was saying, the high priest tore his garments and cried out, "He has blasphemed! What further need have we of witnesses? You have heard the blasphemy. What do you think?"

They all shouted, "He deserves death."

Jesus, the Son of our Heavenly Father, wanted to be tried by the courts of men. Let us love him, who for our salvation became man, suffered and died....

Peter Is Sorry for His Sin, but Judas Despairs

Meanwhile Peter had succeeded in getting into the high priest's inner courtyard. Because the night was cold, he had gone near the fire to warm himself. Soldiers and servants were gathered around the fire, and suddenly one of the servants recognized Peter and said, "You also were with Jesus, the Galilean."

Instead of proudly admitting the truth, Peter denied his Master, saying, "I do not know what you are saying." He wanted to get away from that situation and, in fact, he was just leaving when another maidservant said to those around, "This man also was with Jesus of Nazareth!"

"I do not know the man!" repeated Peter.

The people in the courtyard surrounded him, then, and began to declare, "Surely you are one of them, for even your speech gives you away."

For the third time, Peter swore that he did not know Christ. Just then a cock crowed, and Peter remembered the Master's words to him: "Before a cock crows twice, you will deny me three times." He was about to leave when he saw Jesus, who at that moment was coming from Caiphas' court. The Lord turned and looked upon Peter, and his compassionate glance filled Peter's soul with repentant sorrow. Going out, he wept bitterly.

Meanwhile Judas, when he saw that Jesus was condemned to death, felt bad and brought back the thirty pieces of silver to the chief priests and the elders saying: "I have sinned in betraying innocent blood." But they said, "What is that to us? See to it yourself." So Judas threw the pieces into the Temple, and went out and hanged himself.

Because he was afraid of what others might say or do, Peter denied Jesus. He thus committed a very serious sin. But God can forgive every sin, when someone is sorry. Peter was sorry for his sin, and he cried over it with all his heart. Judas, instead, did not believe in the love and mercy of God. That was why he despaired.

Jesus Tells Pilate That He Is a King

Because Palestine was ruled by Rome at that time, Jesus was then brought to Pilate, the Roman governor. It was early morning.

"Are you a king?" asked Pilate.

"Yes," answered Jesus, "but my kingdom is not of this world".

Now Herod, the king of Galilee, was in Jerusalem in those days, for the feast. As soon as Pilate found out that Jesus was a Galilean, he sent him to Herod. Herod was very glad to see Jesus, for he hoped to see him work some miracle. But Jesus did not even look at that king, because Herod was a very sinful man. So Herod treated Jesus with scorn and made fun of him. He put a bright robe on Jesus to make people think he was crazy and then sent him back to Pilate.

It was the custom to free one prisoner at the time of the passover feast. Pilate tried to use this custom in order to save Jesus, whom he saw was innocent. Pilate asked the people whether they wanted him to free Jesus, who had always done good, or Barabbas, a thief and murderer. Urged on by the priests, the people shouted back, "Release to us Barabbas!"

"Then what shall I do with Jesus, who is called Christ?"

"Crucify him!"

"Why, what evil has he done?"

"Crucify him! Crucify him!" yelled that bloodthirsty mob.

Pilate washed his hands in front of all the people, declaring that he was innocent of the blood of that just Man.

"His blood be on us and on our children!" the people answered.

Trying again to make the mob feel sorry for Jesus, Pilate had him scourged, that is, whipped. The scourging was horrible. The strokes seemed without number; they went on and on. Pieces of the innocent flesh of Jesus were whipped into the air and his blood streamed onto the ground.

Not satisfied, the Roman soldiers then made a crown of very sharp thorns and put it on Jesus' head. They placed a reed in his hand and a purple rag around his shoulders to make fun of him.

"Hail, king of the Jews!" they shouted with laughter, kneeling down in front of him.

When Pilate saw Jesus in such a sad condition, he felt sorry for him and showed him to the crowd, saying, "Behold the Man!"

"Crucify him! Crucify him!"

"Take him yourselves and crucify him!" Pilate said to them.

But the Jews did not have the authority to do that. So they shouted, "If you do not crucify this Man, you are no friend of Caesar...."

Pilate became afraid at these words. Caesar might have him punished. He sat down on the judgment-seat and pronounced the death sentence.

Jesus was not recognized as a king. Even today many people do not want to recognize Jesus as their King. Let us pray in the Our Father: "Thy kingdom come!" One who believes in Jesus Christ will forever reign with him in his kingdom—heaven!

Jesus Carries the Cross to Calvary

Then Jesus' own clothes were put back on him. Two tree trunks in the form of a cross were laid on his shoulders, and he was made to start out for Calvary.

Jesus was exhausted. He had lost a great amount of blood. His body was one great wound and he had not had a moment's rest. His strength failed him more than once, and he fell beneath the cross.

Fearing that he might die on the way, the soldiers forced a certain man named Simon of Cyrene to carry the cross after our Lord.

On this sorrowful way of the cross, Jesus met the Blessed Mother, who was suffering all her Son's pain and sorrow in her own soul. Other women from Jerusalem were also there, weeping at seeing Jesus in such a sad condition. Our Lord comforted them and told them that he was suffering for our sins.

Let us think of Jesus carrying his cross. He seems to be telling us: "Without a cross, you cannot enter heaven. He who wishes to follow me, let him deny himself, take up his cross, and follow me."

Jesus Dies on the Cross

A great crowd of people followed Jesus to Calvary. Upon reaching the place of execution, the soldiers stripped Jesus of his garments and stretched him out on the cross. They hammered nails into his hands and feet to hold him fast to the cross. Then they raised the cross and dropped it into the hole they had dug for it. Behold Jesus, suspended between heaven and earth, hanging by three spikes, a victim offered for the sins of all men!

Two thieves were crucified with Jesus, one at his right and one at his left. At the top of his cross a sign was posted: *Jesus of Nazareth, King of the Jews.*

It was about noon when Jesus was crucified. The sun was darkened and night fell over the face of the earth. At the foot of the cross, all the enemies of Jesus continued to insult him. But he offered to his Father the prayer of forgiveness: "Father, forgive them, for they do not know what they are doing!"

The Blessed Mother, St. John and the holy women had accompanied Jesus to Calvary.

When Jesus looked down from the cross, he saw that little group of people so dear to his heart. To his mother he said, "Woman, behold your son!" And to John, "Behold your mother!" From that moment on, John considered the Mother of Jesus as his mother. John represented all mankind, so Mary then became the spiritual mother of all men.

After having suffered for three terrible hours on the cross, Jesus cried out, "I thirst!" He was torn by a burning thirst and was suffering greatly in spirit, too. His thirst was a thirst for souls.

Death was nearing. Jesus knew that the Redemption was about to be completed and he said, "It is finished!" Then in a loud voice, he cried, "Father, into your hands, I entrust my spirit!" And bowing his head, he died. The great sacrifice was over. It was three o'clock in the afternoon of Good Friday. And behold, as soon as Jesus had died, the earth shook as by a great earthquake; rocks were split apart; many tombs opened and the bodies of the saints arose. The veil of the Temple was torn in two from top to bottom.

When the centurion on guard saw all that had happened, he exclaimed, "This was truly the Son of God!" The other people there were also very frightened and they went down Calvary hill beating their breasts.

The friends of the Lord approached the cross. Carefully they took down the body and placed it in the arms of Jesus' sorrowful mother. Then they hurriedly embalmed it, wrapped it in a winding sheet, and placed it in a sepulcher or tomb. Jesus' enemies sealed the sepulcher and sent a group of soldiers to guard it.

Jesus Christ suffered and died as man. His sufferings, however, being also those of a Divine Person, have an infinite value: "Through his sufferings we were all healed." Jesus endured all this—his bitter agony of soul, his bloody sweat, his cruel scourging, his crowning with thorns, his journey to Calvary and his death on the cross—to show his love for men

and to repay God for the offense of Adam and Eve. Only God could make up for the sin of our first parents and all our sins.

As soon as Jesus breathed his last, his soul went into limbo, where the souls of all the good people, both pagan and Hebrew, who had died up until that time, were waiting for him. Jesus went there to tell them that the Redemption had been fulfilled and that the moment of their release was coming. The soul of Jesus remained in limbo for three days.

We believe in our Lord Jesus Christ...
who suffered under Pontius Pilate —
the Lamb of God bearing on himself the sins of the world —
and died for us on the cross,
saving us by his redeeming blood....
His Kingdom will have no end.

Credo of the People of God

Jesus Rises from the Dead

The Victory of Easter

The entrance to Jesus' tomb had been closed with a heavy stone and sealed by the guards.

And when the Sabbath was over (for on that day the Hebrews were forbidden to do any work) Mary Magdalene, Mary the mother of James the Less, and Salome (mother of James the Great and John), bought spices, that they might go and complete the anointing of the body of Jesus, which they had done only hurriedly on Friday. These women had been serving the Redeemer for some time. They had gone with him on his various apostolic journeys, giving him needed care and attention. They had followed him to Calvary, and now had bought spices to pay their last honor to the body of the Lord.

They came to the tomb very early, when the sun had just risen. And they were saying to one another, "Who will roll the stone back from the entrance of the tomb for us?" And looking up they saw that the stone had been rolled back. Timid and fearful, they entered the tomb. And what a vision they saw! A shining young man, clothed in white garments, sat waiting for them. They were frightened, but he said to them, "Do not be afraid. You are looking for Jesus of Nazareth, who was crucified. He has risen; he is not here. See the place where they laid him."

At dawn on Sunday morning, the soul of Jesus had been reunited with his body, to the self-same body as before, which became alive and glorious.

After having announced to the pious women that Jesus had truly risen, the angel added: "Go, tell his disciples and

Peter that he goes before you into Galilee; there you shall see him, as he told you." How privileged those women were! They were given the honor of announcing the glorious resurrection of Christ!

Jesus died as man; he rose again by his own power as God. The resurrection is the greatest proof that Jesus Christ is God.

Christ truly arose from the dead. We are certain of this for several reasons. The sepulcher was found empty. Who could have taken away Jesus' body? Not his enemies, who had placed a guard around him, nor his apostles, who were in hiding because they were afraid. Also, he himself remained on earth after his resurrection for forty days during which he proved, with many apparitions, that he had truly risen from the dead.

Jesus appeared to his most holy mother (the Gospel does not mention this apparition, but it is certain), to Mary Magdalene, to the holy women, to Peter, to the two disciples of Emmaus, to the apostles in the Cenacle when Thomas was absent, to the apostles in the Cenacle when Thomas was present, to over two hundred disciples who were gathered together, to St. James, to the apostles on Lake Genesareth, and finally, on the day of his ascension, to a large crowd who witnessed his last miracle.

In these apparitions, Jesus continued to instruct the apostles; he gave them the power to forgive sin and preach the Gospel to the whole world; he confirmed St. Peter as head of his Church.

Jesus Gives the Apostles the Power To Forgive Sins

The apostles were gathered behind closed doors for fear of the Jews. Jesus appeared twice in their midst in the Cenacle: in the first apparition, which took place on the very evening of Easter, the Savior confirmed the apostles in the mission of preaching the Gospel to all creatures and gave them the power to forgive sins. In the second apparition, which took place eight days afterwards, he made Thomas touch him with his hands to prove that he had truly risen.

In the apparition of Easter evening, Jesus entered the Cenacle through closed doors and said: "Peace be to you!" The glorified body of the Risen Christ could move very rapidly; it did not need food or sleep; and it could pass through other objects. This was why he could enter the Cenacle through closed doors. To assure the apostles that he was not appearing in spirit only, but that it was really he in flesh and blood, Jesus showed them his hands with the marks of the nails and the wound in his side. The disciples rejoiced at the sight of the Lord and believed that he had risen.

Jesus repeated a second time the heavenly greeting: "Peace be to you!" Have you ever stopped to consider what a wonderful thing peace of heart is? Cain, after having killed Abel, never found peace again. Judas, after having betrayed Jesus, did not have peace. So it is with all sinners. True peace is found only in the friendship of God.

By wishing them true peace, Jesus prepared the apostles for their great mission: "As the Father has sent me, I also send you." The Father sent Jesus to save mankind; and Jesus sent his apostles and their successors to continue his work of salvation until the end of the world. Having pronounced these words, Jesus breathed upon them and added: "Receive the Holy Spirit; whose sins you shall forgive, they are forgiven them; and whose sins you shall retain, they are retained"

At that moment, the sacrament of penance was instituted. This is the means, after baptism, of obtaining pardon for our sins.

When we receive the sacrament of penance it is Jesus himself who forgives our sins through the absolution of the priest.

Jesus Makes Peter the Head of His Church

Not long after these events, Simon Peter and six other disciples went fishing on the Sea of Galilee. All night long they caught nothing. When the day was breaking, however, Jesus stood on the beach; yet the disciples could not see that it was Jesus. Then Jesus said to them, "Young men, have you any fish?"

They answered him, "No."

He said to them, "Cast the net to the right of the boat, and you will find them."

They threw out the net, therefore, and now they could not pull it up because of the great number of fish in it.

John, the disciple whom Jesus loved, said to Peter, "It is the Lord."

When he heard this, Simon Peter threw himself into the sea and swam toward Jesus. The other disciples followed him in the boat. When they had reached the shore, they saw a fire ready and fish laid upon it and bread. Jesus said to them, "Come and have breakfast." And he gave them bread and fish. When they had eaten, Jesus said to Simon Peter, "Simon, son of John, do you love me more than these do?"

Peter replied, "Yes, Lord. You know that I love you."

"Feed my lambs," Jesus said. Then he repeated the same question. "Simon, son of John, do you love me?"

"Yes, Lord," Peter replied again. "You know that I love you."

Again Jesus said, "Feed my lambs." And a third time the Master asked, "Simon, son of John, do you love me?"

Peter felt sad because Jesus had again asked him, "Do you love me?"

"Lord," he said, "you know all things; you know that I love you!"

This time Jesus told him, "Feed my sheep"

Another time Jesus had said to Peter: "You are Peter (which means rock), and on this rock, I will build my Church. And I will give to you the keys of the kingdom...." Now, after the resurrection, Jesus commanded Peter to *feed* his lambs and his *sheep;* he meant that Peter was to be the highest authority over the faithful and the shepherds (priests and bishops) of the Church.

St. Peter is great because our Lord Jesus Christ gave him such great authority and also because he had so much faith and was so generous in the service of God.

After preaching the Gospel in different places and converting many souls, St. Peter founded the Church in Rome which he governed until the end of his life. From Rome he ruled all the faithful, and wrote to them two beautiful letters which showed how much he loved them all.

Under the Emperor Nero, St. Peter was put in prison and then was cruelly martyred. He was crucified upside down. There on Vatican hill, where St. Peter shed his blood for his beloved Jesus, the great Basilica of St. Peter stands today.

Peter was the first Pope. After him, other Popes continued to guide the Church with a sure hand, and they will keep on guiding it until the end of the world. The Church is often compared to Peter's little boat; it is sometimes struck by heavy winds and fierce storms caused by the devil, but it will always sail on securely over the rough waves until it reaches port, because the Lord said, "the gates of hell shall not prevail against it".

Christ from death is risen,
our new life obtaining,
Have mercy, victor King, ever reigning!
Alleluia.

Liturgy

160

Jesus Returns to the Father

Now ended were the forty beautiful days in which the risen Jesus had appeared to his disciples and lovingly talked with them. Now he was to return to his Father and the glory and delights of heaven. He told them all—apostles and disciples—to meet in Jerusalem. Then, before ascending to heaven, the Savior explained to his followers that it had been necessary for him to suffer and to rise from the dead, and that in his name, they should preach penance and the forgiveness of sin.

He then told them to stay in Jerusalem and prayerfully await the coming of the Holy Spirit, who would enlighten their minds and strengthen their hearts: "You shall receive power when the Holy Spirit comes upon you, and you shall be witnesses for me in Jerusalem and in all Judea and Samaria and even to the very ends of the earth. And behold, I am with you all days, even to the very end of the world."

After giving them his last instructions, Jesus led his apostles and disciples to the top of Mount Olivet. At the foot of that same mountain, he had begun his passion, and now from its summit, he was going to ascend gloriously into heaven.

Before leaving his beloved followers, Jesus lifted his hands and blessed them all. Then he began to rise from the ground and slowly ascended higher and higher, until a cloud surrounded him and hid him from the apostles' view. They stood as still as statues, their eyes fixed on the spot where their Lord had disappeared.

Through his own power Jesus had risen from the dead and through his own power he ascended into heaven. He ascended with his soul and glorified body. As a victorious King he took possession of his Kingdom which he had won by his passion and death. He was accompanied by the joyful souls of the good people of the Old Testament, and was welcomed with hymns of praise by the choirs of angels.

The disciples were overjoyed at the glorious triumph of Jesus and at his promise to be with them always. They went back to Jerusalem and were continually in the Temple praising and blessing God.

Jesus has two thrones: one of glory in heaven, and the other of love on earth. In heaven he reveals himself in the full splendor of his divinity, forming, together with the Father and the Holy Spirit, the joy of the blessed. On earth his glory is veiled by the eucharistic Species, which let us approach him without fear and to nourish our soul with him.

Jesus ascended into heaven to enter into his glory and to prepare a place for us. He stayed on earth in the Eucharist to fight beside us, to receive our worship, and above all to continue the Sacrifice of Calvary with the Mass and to give us a foretaste of future glory through Holy Communion.

The Lord Jesus will visibly return to earth at the end of the world, not humble and hidden, but *in the full splendor of his glory,* as he himself said, and as the angels repeated on ascension day to the apostles who continued to stare up at the cloud which had hidden the Master from their sight: "Men of Galilee, why do you stand looking up to heaven? This Jesus who has been taken up from you into heaven, shall come in the same way as you have seen him going up to heaven"

No one knows when the end of the world will come, nor when the General Judgment will take place. Jesus revealed to us only the signs which will come before it. The General Judgment will mark the greatest glorification of Christ, the victory of the good and the humiliating defeat of the wicked.

O Almighty God, your Son, our Savior, ascended into heaven. May we always think of our heavenly home.

Ascension Liturgy

162

The Descent of the Holy Spirit

After Jesus ascended into heaven, the apostles returned to Jerusalem. In the Cenacle, or upper room, they prayed and awaited the coming of the Holy Spirit. With the apostles were Mary Most Holy, the holy women, the disciples and relatives of Jesus. How wonderful it must have been to be in the company of the Blessed Virgin! What great value her prayers had!

The fiftieth day after Jesus' resurrection arrived. The Hebrew feast of *Pentecost* fell on this day, and Jews had come to Jerusalem from many lands to give thanks to God.

On the very day of Pentecost, at about nine o'clock in the morning, there suddenly came a sound from heaven, as if a strong wind were blowing. It filled the whole house where the apostles and disciples of the Lord were recollected in prayer. At the same time there appeared to them parted tongues as of fire, which could be seen settling down upon each one of them. And they were all filled with the Holy Spirit and began to speak in foreign languages.

Now when this sound was heard, crowds gathered at the Cenacle and were greatly bewildered because each person heard the apostles speaking in the language of his own distant country. The apostles spoke of the wonderful works of God, and the amazed people kept asking one another, "What does this mean?" Then Peter, as the head of the Church, spoke out boldly to the crowd about Jesus.

Peter's words filled the hearts of many of his listeners, and they asked the apostles: "Brothers, what shall we do?"

"Be sorry and be baptized every one of you in the name of Jesus Christ for the forgiveness of your sins; and you will receive the gift of the Holy Spirit."

That day, about three thousand people were baptized and became followers of Jesus.

When the Holy Spirit came, he had transformed Jesus' disciples from worldly men into saints. He had changed their ignorance to wisdom, and their fear to bravery. He had given them the gifts of tongues, miracles and prophecy.

The Holy Spirit with his seven gifts descended upon us, too, in baptism and in confirmation, and he continuously breathes upon our souls. In his action the Holy Spirit offers each soul the graces it needs, corresponding to its desires and its mission in the world. Do you know what dispositions are necessary to receive the gifts of the Spirit of God in abundance? Jesus told us: "If anyone loves me, he will keep my word, and my Father will love him, and we will come to him and make our home with him."

"He who does not love me," continued Jesus, "does not keep my words".

Thus our Lord clearly describes those who do not love him: they are the people who do not observe his Commandments. The words of Jesus are the words of the heavenly Father. He who does not love Jesus is not loved by the Father, is not visited by his Holy Spirit, and is left to the devil. What misfortune!

The First Christians

The three thousand Hebrews who received baptism on Pentecost brought the doctrine of salvation back to their own lands with them.

In Jerusalem the preaching of the apostles and the miracles they worked made such a deep impression that the number of believers grew to five thousand. All these listened eagerly to the preaching of the apostles, who repeated Christ's teachings. They all assisted at the breaking of the bread—the Holy Mass. They lived in a holy unity of spirit and helped one another in their needs.

Not having any large buildings, the apostles used to gather the faithful in the porches of the Temple of Jerusalem. There they gave them instructions. The number of the faithful kept growing and growing.

Our Lord had told the apostles to preach the Gospel to every creature. So, even though they did their first preaching in Jerusalem and Palestine, they were already looking forward to going farther. The Church is a missionary Church. Missionaries still go into the whole world to proclaim the word of Jesus, as he himself told them to do.

How can you help the missions?

St. Stephen Dies for the Faith

The number of Christians increased so much that the apostles could not themselves handle all their duties as shepherds of the faithful. So they gathered the Christians together and told them, "Brothers, choose from among your group seven men of good reputation, full of the Holy Spirit and of wisdom, to help us in matters of ministration."

Stephen was one of the men the faithful chose. After praying, the apostles laid their hands upon the seven and asked for the abundance of the Holy Spirit to come down upon them. These men were called deacons, and their work was to help the apostles, especially in giving money to the poor.

Of those seven deacons, the one who showed the most love for God and souls was Stephen. Full of the Holy Spirit and of courage, he worked great miracles among the people. Some enemies of the Christians, who had seen Stephen's miracles and knew how holy he was, decided to argue with him. Inspired by God, Stephen spoke with such wisdom that his enemies were amazed and could not find words to answer him.

They were very much embarrassed because of this, and in their hatred of Stephen they decided to put him to death. They dragged him before the religious court, and paid false witnesses to lie about him, saying that they had heard him blaspheme against Moses and the Temple.

"Are their charges true?" demanded the high priest.

Right there in front of them all, Stephen made a long, beautiful reply. He recalled the history of the people of Israel. He spoke of how God had many times promised the Savior through the prophets. He said that the Savior had indeed come into the world, but that they had had him crucified.

The crowd gritted their teeth in anger. Full of the Holy Spirit, Stephen looked up to heaven. The skies opened up before his eyes and he was able to see the glory of God.

"Behold!" he exclaimed, "I see the heavens opened and the Son of Man standing at the right hand of God."

Beside themselves with anger, his hearers stopped their ears to shut out the sound of his voice. Shouting furiously, they

leaped upon him to kill him. As though he were a blasphemer, they dragged him outside the city, and then hurled upon him stone after stone. "Lord Jesus, receive my spirit," prayed the saint. Then he fell to his knees, raised his arms toward heaven and cried, "Lord, forgive them this sin!" With that, he dropped to the ground, asleep in the Lord.

St. Stephen was the first martyr, the first to give his life for Jesus. Let us often think of this brave saint and try to imitate his courage and love for his faith.

The Conversion and Apostolate of St. Paul

St. Paul was one of the greatest men the world has ever known. He was the apostle who worked more than anyone else in the Church. He was born in the city of Tarsus, in Asia Minor. His parents were very good Jews who belonged to the tribe of Benjamin. He was named Saul, and he was very smart and full of energy, even though he was never too well. Saul went to the schools of his city and was an excellent student and wonderful speaker. He was very learned in the Bible. When he left the synagogue schools, he went to Jerusalem, where he had the famous rabbi, Gamaliel, for his teacher. He received the title, "Doctor of the Law," and then left Jerusalem, probably just at the time that Jesus was beginning his public life, for it seems that he never knew or spoke with Jesus.

Saul was very obedient to the Hebrew religion, and when he heard people talking about the new Christian religion, he was very much disgusted. He thought it was all false. So with terrible zeal, he took part in the stoning of St. Stephen, the first martyr, and in all the persecutions against the Christians. In fact, he excelled everyone in his hatred of the Christians. The Acts of the Apostles says that Saul was tormenting the Church. He would enter one house after another, dragging out men and women, and putting them in prison. He had made up his mind to destroy the Christian religion, and he was doing his best to keep his resolution! But God made this fiercest of all the Church's persecutors into the greatest apostle!

168

Saul went to the high priest at Jerusalem, who gave him written permission to put into prison all the Christians in the city of Damascus. But, as he galloped full speed toward Damascus, he was suddenly blinded by a bright light which knocked him to the ground. From out of that light came a strong, kind voice calling out to him: "Saul, Saul, why are you persecuting me?"

Amazed, Saul asked, "Who are you Lord?" And back came the reply: "I am Jesus whom you are persecuting. It is hard for you to kick against the goad" (this meant: it is hard for you to resist my grace).

"Lord, what will you have me do?" Saul asked at once, trembling and amazed.

"Arise and go into the city, and you will be told what you must do," came the answer. Now those who had come with Saul were unable to speak, so astonished were they. They had heard the words but had seen no one. Saul arose and discovered that he could see nothing. He had become blind. He was led into Damascus, where he stayed three days without eating, until a disciple of the Lord named Ananias went to him to baptize him, at the command of Jesus. Right then, something like scales fell from Saul's eyes; he recovered his sight and was filled with the Holy Spirit. He stayed with the Christians of Damascus for several days and began at once to preach in the Jewish synagogues that Jesus was truly the Son of God. Those who heard him were amazed and asked one another, "Isn't this the man who was persecuting the Christians in Jerusalem and who came here to put them all in prison?"

The conversion of St. Paul is the most amazing one in history. After his conversion, Saul went into the desert to pray, think and do penance. During those three years he spent alone in the desert, Saul was taught more about the truths of faith by Jesus himself. When he returned to Jerusalem and talked with Peter and the other apostles, his doctrine was fully approved.

Yet Saul did not begin his great missionary journeys at once. For another seven years he waited, working quietly, unknown to most. Jesus had told Ananias that Saul was a chosen instrument to carry Christianity among nations and kings and the people of Israel. Jesus had also said that Saul would have to suffer for the name of Christ. Therefore, after almost ten years of preparing very well, Saul began his great work of converting pagans, at God's command. When he worked among the pagans, Saul used a Roman name, Paul.

He made four famous missionary journeys. After his third journey, his enemies managed to have him put into prison. Paul, however, was a Roman citizen, and he refused to go on trial in Jerusalem. He appealed to Caesar, the Roman emperor. Paul had long desired to go to Rome, and at last he had his chance to go, but as a prisoner. This was his fourth journey. He was shipwrecked on the Island of Malta, but reached Rome safely and remained there for two years as a prisoner.

During that time, he preached the Gospel to the Romans and wrote letters full of wisdom and grace.

Paul was set free for a while, but when the first big persecution began, he and St. Peter were both arrested. They were put in a horrible prison, called the Mamertine prison, and then martyred. St. Paul was beheaded outside Rome. That was in the year 67 A.D.

During his missionary life, Paul had traveled throughout almost the whole known world. He ended his adventurous life by shedding his blood for Christ in the capital city of the world. Yet not even when he died did he stop preaching Christ, because the fourteen letters he wrote have done immense good down through the centuries. Parts of them are read almost every day in the Mass.

St. Paul is called the Apostle of the Gentiles because he worked especially for the conversion of the Gentiles, or pagans. He is a real model of an apostle. Nothing could stop him in his missionary zeal. In him the love of Christ and souls was a fire that never went out.

In a letter to the Corinthians, St. Paul listed the sufferings he had had to bear: "From the Jews five times I received thirty-nine lashes. Three times I was scourged, once I was stoned, three times I suffered shipwreck, a night and a day I was adrift

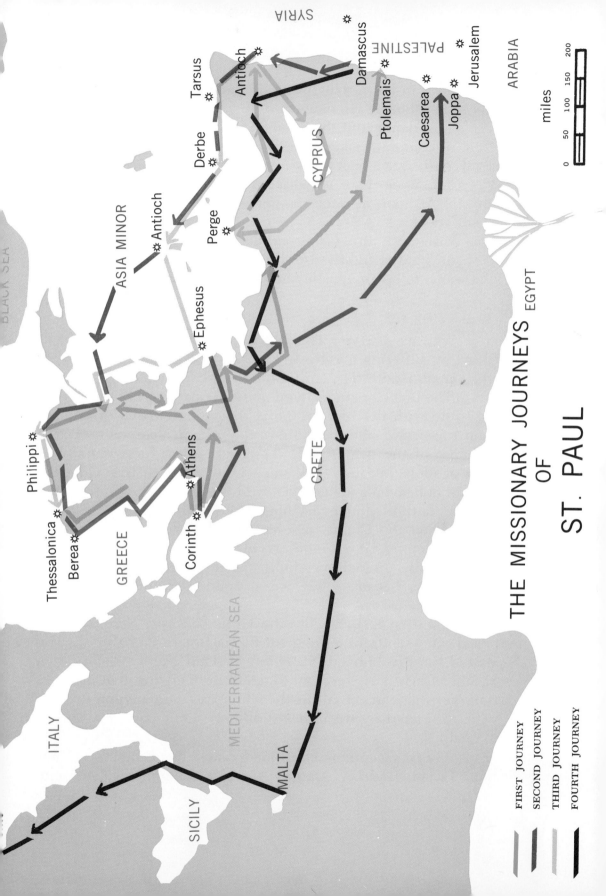

THE MISSIONARY JOURNEYS
OF
ST. PAUL

BLACK SEA

SYRIA

PALESTINE

ARABIA

Damascus

Jerusalem

Antioch

Tarsus

Ptolemais

Caesarea

Joppa

Derbe

CYPRUS

Perge

ASIA MINOR

Antioch

Ephesus

GREECE

Philippi

Thessalonica

Berea

Athens

Corinth

CRETE

MEDITERRANEAN SEA

ITALY

SICILY

MALTA

EGYPT

miles

0   50   100   150   200

FIRST JOURNEY

SECOND JOURNEY

THIRD JOURNEY

FOURTH JOURNEY

on the sea; in journeying often, in dangers from floods, in dangers from robbers,...in dangers in the city, in dangers in the wilderness, in dangers in the sea,... in hunger and thirst, in fastings often, in cold and nakedness. Besides those outer things, there is my daily great worry, the care of all the churches!" Now, do you think St. Paul got discouraged over all those troubles? Oh, no! As soon as each danger was over, he would go right ahead speaking of Jesus Christ and converting people to the true Faith with the same enthusiasm as before!

St. Paul is rightly called *the great Apostle*, and everyone who wants to be an apostle should imitate him.

The Martyrs

Who are martyrs? They are people who prove their faith in Christ by suffering greatly and by dying at the hands of people who hate the Faith. The early Church had many martyrs.

The first Christians lived quiet, good lives. They had nothing to do with the bloody sports that great crowds of Romans went to see. Nor did they join in the religious ceremonies held in honor of the pagan gods. They refused to burn incense in front of idols, because they adored only the one true God, the Creator of heaven and earth. They loved Jesus Christ, our Savior, and they faithfully did everything he taught us.

When the Christian religion had spread throughout the Roman Empire, the emperors of Rome waged ten terrible persecutions, one after another. They were out to destroy Christianity, because they were afraid it would offend their pagan gods.

The first to persecute the Christians was *Nero*, who accused them of starting the great fire of Rome. Probably, he had started the fire himself. St. Peter, St. Paul and a great number of other Christians were put to death for Christ in that persecution. Terrible ways of killing the Christians were invented. Some were torn apart by wild beasts, others crucified, others burned to death....

The persecutions continued under the Emperors Domitian, Trajan, Hadrian, Marcus Aurelius, Commodus, Septimus

Severus, Decius, Valerian, and especially Diocletian. During Diocletian's persecution, the number of martyrs became impossible to count. Among those whose names we know, St. Sebastian, St. Agnes, St. Dorothy, St. Lucy and St. Anastasia were martyred during this persecution.

Yet, the blood of those martyrs was the seed of new Christians, as the famous saying goes. The more Christianity was persecuted, the more it spread and grew strong. If the Church had not been assisted by the Holy Spirit, it certainly would have been completely destroyed, but the fact is that after about three hundred years of persecution, it came out victorious. The Emperor Constantine at last granted liberty to the Church.

The martyrs were of all ages and all types: old people and children, young men and women, fathers and mothers, rich and poor, learned and unlearned.

St. Pancratius, for example, was only fourteen years old. His father had died a martyr and his mother, Lucina, had brought him up faithful to the religion of Christ.

Brave and quick-thinking, Pancratius was a natural leader and had become a soldier in the army. The other soldiers did not know that he was a Christian.

Whenever he was not on duty, Pancratius brought food and drink to the Christians who were in prison because of their Faith.

Then one day some soldiers caught him comforting a martyr as he lay dying. "Yes, I, too, am a Christian," Pancratius said. He was put in prison at once. Even when the Emperor Diocletian tried to persuade him to give up his Faith, the boy would not do so.

Pancratius was led through the city of Rome, with soldiers whipping him as he walked. Among those who followed him was his mother, who prayed that he would die a good Christian, as he had lived. And Pancratius did so. At the place of his martyrdom, he knelt down and placed his head on a stone block. While the executioner raised his sword, Pancratius asked God to forgive those who were putting him to death.

Thus, like so many glorious martyrs before him, Pancratius gave up his life in order to remain faithful to Christ.

The martyrs are wonderful models for boys and girls who dare, even today! to be courageous in the army of Christ the King.

We believe in the Holy Spirit,
who was sent by Christ
after his resurrection and ascension to the Father.
He gives light, life, protection and guidance
to the Church.

Credo of the People of God

Daughters of St. Paul

MASSACHUSETTS
50 St. Paul's Ave., Jamaica Plain, Boston, MA 02130; **617-522-8911.**
172 Tremont Street, Boston, MA 02111; **617-426-5464; 617-426-4230.**
NEW YORK
78 Fort Place, Staten Island, NY 10301; **718-447-5071; 718-447-5086.**
59 East 43rd Street, New York, NY 10017; **212-986-7580.**
625 East 187th Street, Bronx, NY 10458; **212-584-0440.**
525 Main Street, Buffalo, NY 14203; **716-847-6044.**
NEW JERSEY
Hudson Mall—Route 440 and Communipaw Ave.,
Jersey City, NJ 07304; **201-433-7740.**
CONNECTICUT
202 Fairfield Ave., Bridgeport, CT 06604; **203-335-9913.**
OHIO
2105 Ontario Street (at Prospect Ave.), Cleveland, OH 44115;
216-621-9427.
616 Walnut Street, Cincinnati, OH 45202; **513-421-5733; 513-721-5059.**
PENNSYLVANIA
1719 Chestnut Street, Philadelphia, PA 19103; **215-568-2638.**
VIRGINIA
1025 King Street, Alexandria, VA 22314;   **703-549-3806.**
SOUTH CAROLINA
243 King Street, Charleston, SC 29401; **803-577-0175.**
FLORIDA
2700 Biscayne Blvd., Miami, FL 33137; **305-573-1618; 305-573-1624.**
LOUISIANA
4403 Veterans Memorial Blvd., Metairie, LA 70006; **504-887-7631;
504-887-0113.**
423 Main Street, Baton Rouge, LA 70802; **504-343-4057; 504-381-9485.**
MISSOURI
1001 Pine Street (at North 10th), St. Louis, MO 63101; **314-621-0346;**

ILLINOIS
172 North Michigan Ave., Chicago, IL 60601; **312-346-4228; 312-346-3240.**
TEXAS
114 Main Plaza, San Antonio, TX 78205; **512-224-8101**
CALIFORNIA
1570 Fifth Ave. (at Cedar St.), San Diego, CA 92101; **619-232-1442.**
46 Geary Street, San Francisco, CA 94108; **415-781-5180.**
WASHINGTON
2301 Second Ave., Seattle, WA 98121; **206-441-3300**
HAWAII
1143 Bishop Street, Honolulu, HI 96813; **808-521-2731.**
ALASKA
750 West 5th Ave., Anchorage, AK 99501; **907-272-8183.**

CANADA
3022 Dufferin Street, Toronto 395, Ontario, Canada.

MORE BIBLE STORIES

from St. Paul Editions!
Write today for a complete price list

Daughters of St. Paul   50 St. Paul's Ave.   Boston, MA 02130
or from the Daughters of St. Paul, St. Paul Catholic
Book and Audio-Visual Center nearest you!

Jesus in the Gospel

Companion volume to **The Adventures of Peter and Paul.** Bright illustrations accompany this life of Christ which uses the unified Gospel texts...right from the New Testament! (Ages 10-14) 304 pages — CH0288

Adventures of Peter and Paul

This book narrates the travels, the preaching, the risks and the rewards of the two Apostles, St. Peter—the first Pope; and St. Paul—the first and greatest missionary. The faith they received from Jesus Christ Himself they shared with all the then-known world. (Ages 10-14). 120 pages — CH0015

The Bible for Young People

This dramatically illustrated **New Testament** in full color will make the discovery of the treasures of Sacred Scripture an enjoyable, unforgettable experience for young people (**Ages 9-13**). 142 pages — CH0080

Bible for Children

God's message is one of saving love, and it unfolds admirably in the pages of this book. Covering both **Old and New Testaments** of the Bible, it majestically sets forth the more important happenings in the history of salvation. Their meaning is also explained in the light of recent biblical studies. Biblical maps are included; illustrations are in 2 and 4 colors (**Ages 8-12**). 182 pages — CH0070

The Teachings and Miracles of Jesus

Some of the best-known teachings and miracles of our Lord are retold in this volume for young people. Jesus has an answer to every question; He has words of everlasting life. His tender love for people and His divine power will strike unforgettable images on the minds and hearts of youth to aid them to work for His Kingdom (Ages 9-13). 136 pages — CH0690

If you like to read, you'll love

MY FRIEND

magazine!

MY FRIEND is the ideal monthly magazine for boys and girls between the ages of 6 and 12 especially.

MY FRIEND comes out every month during the school year, so you'll receive 10 copies during the year.

MY FRIEND has 32 colorful pages of fun and learning!

* Bible Stories * Sports * Contests
* Projects * Science Articles * Lives of the Saints

**Write today for an order blank
for your subscription to**

MY FRIEND

DON'T MISS AN ISSUE!

This book was printed by the Daughters of St. Paul. They are sister-apostles of today who use all the most modern media—press, films, radio, television, cassettes, video cassettes and records—to spread the Gospel of Jesus throughout the world.

If you are a girl between the ages of 14 and 26, and would like more information on the life and mission of the Daughters of St. Paul, write to:

Vocation Directress
Daughters of St. Paul
50 St. Paul's Avenue
Jamaica Plain, MA 02130
617-522-8911

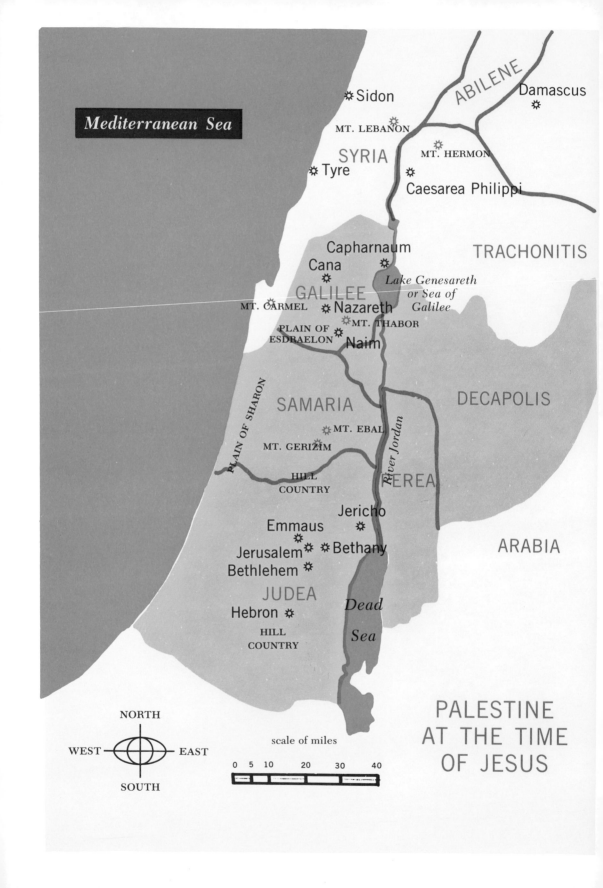

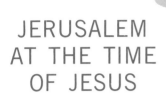

JERUSALEM
AT THE TIME
OF JESUS

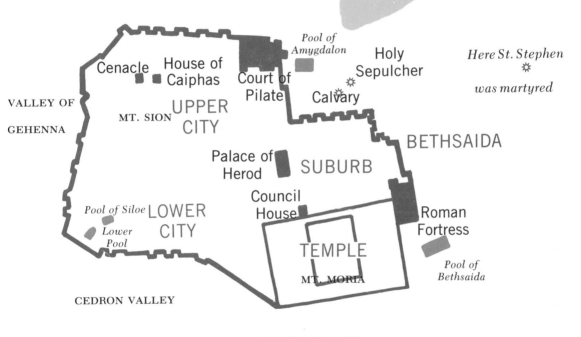

Pool of
Amygdalon

Holy
Sepulcher

Here St. Stephen
was martyred

Cenacle   House of
Caiphas

Court of
Pilate

Calvary

VALLEY OF

GEHENNA

MT. SION   UPPER
CITY

BETHSAIDA

Palace of
Herod

SUBURB

Council
House

Pool of Siloe LOWER
CITY

Lower
Pool

Roman
Fortress

TEMPLE

MT. MORIA

Pool of
Bethsaida

CEDRON VALLEY

CEDRON VALLEY

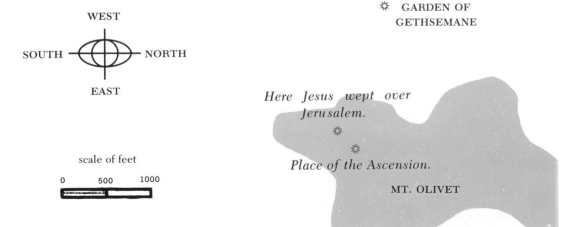

GARDEN OF
GETHSEMANE

WEST

SOUTH   NORTH

EAST

Here Jesus wept over
Jerusalem.

Place of the Ascension.

MT. OLIVET

scale of feet

0   500   1000